Minimum Wage Regulation in Retail Trade

Minimum Wage Regulation in Retail Trade

Belton M. Fleisher

American Enterprise Institute for Public Policy Research
Washington and London

Belton M. Fleisher is professor of economics at the Ohio State University. He is the coauthor of a textbook in labor economics, *Labor Economics: Theory, Evidence, and Policy* (2nd edition, 1980), and the author of *The Economics of Delinquency* (1966) and of numerous articles in professional journals.

Library of Congress Cataloging in Publication Data

Fleisher, Belton M
Minimum wage regulation in retail trade.

(AEI studies ; 307)
Bibliography: p.
1. Wages—Retail trade employees—United States.
I. Title. II. Series: American Enterprise Institute for Public Policy Research. AEI studies ; 307.
KF3505.R3F55 344.73′012813811 80-39895

ISBN 0-8447-3419-5
ISBN 0-8447-3420-9 (pbk.)

AEI Studies 307

Printed in the United States of America

Contents

List of Tables

List of Figures

Preface

In addition to the support of the American Enterprise Institute for Public Policy Research (AEI), I have benefited from a professional leave grant of Ohio State University and the support of Ohio State University's Instruction and Research Computer Center in carrying out this research. Simon Rottenberg, who headed the AEI minimum wage project, provided valuable advice and assistance. John Peterson kindly let me have access to unpublished data from the U.S. Department of Labor that were invaluable in calculating some of the important statistical series used in this study. I have received advice and comments from Mark Berger, Howard Marvel, J. Huston McCulloch, Donald Parsons, and Jerry Thursby. I benefited greatly from comments received when I presented this research to the labor economics workshop at the University of Chicago. Herschel Kasper read an earlier version of the manuscript and offered helpful comments. Philip G. Cotterill kindly provided some unpublished material from his Ph.D. dissertation. Mark Berger supervised estimation of the standard error for the forecast wage developed in appendix C. James E. Brown and Bradley Kunz were my able and willing research assistants, and Pat Akison provided excellent typing service.

During the early stages of my research, I sought the help and advice of several representatives of the retail trade industry, and I wish to acknowledge their cooperation. They include Edward Borda and Donald White of the American Retail Federation, William Davidson of Management Horizons, Inc., and various executives of Federated Department Stores, the K-Mart Corporation, Montgomery Ward and Company, and Sears, Roebuck and Company, who gave generously of their time and advice. I offer my thanks to all these people.

1

Introduction: Retail Trade and Retail Service

Federal legislation on minimum wage and maximum hours was initially imposed in 1938; the retail trade industry, however, has been covered only since September 3, 1961.[1] The purpose of this report is to describe some of the most important effects of federally imposed wage floors in retail trade on employment, hours of work, and the welfare of workers and the public. Isolating cause-effect relationships between legislative interference in any market and the outcome of the market process requires success in establishing what would have taken place in the absence of the particular legislative changes being studied. The practice of such counterfactual investigation involves a mixture of art and science that most social scientists must master, given the absence of laboratories in which the effects of events of interest can be directly observed.

To understand the impact of minimum wage legislation in retail trade, we must first establish a framework that will permit us to make reasonable estimates about what would have happened in the industry had it not been subject to a wage floor. The first step in approaching this task is to outline briefly the nature of the output of the retail trade industry and the technology used to produce it.

Retail (and wholesale) trade, or distribution, is not an essential economic activity in the same sense as the production of goods in the extremely primitive "Robinson Crusoe" economy used to introduce most of us to our first view of the economic system.[2] For this reason,

[1] Employees of mail order firms, constituting approximately 3 percent of all retail trade nonsupervisory employees, were covered under the initial Fair Labor Standards Act beginning in 1938. This study does not cover workers in eating and drinking establishments.

[2] See Harold Barger, *Distribution's Place in the American Economy since 1869* (Princeton, N.J.: Princeton University Press, 1955).

some social commentators often give the impression that retail trade, as characterized by the middleman, is not essential to contemporary economic welfare, and indeed is an unfortunate obstacle preventing consumers from reaping the full value of the incomes they earn. Nothing could be further from the truth, because the extreme specialization of function, or division of labor, that is responsible for the high standard of living Americans enjoy could not be sustained without middlemen to facilitate trade between specialized firms and individuals.

A Simple View of Retail Trade, Household Production, and Consumption

In all contemporary societies with any degree of economic freedom, each individual or household faces the dual problem of allocating available time between producing goods or services that others will use and producing commodities for its own direct benefit, or consumption. Of course, the second activity would be impossible without the first. Unless we produce something valued by others, we are unable to purchase goods and services we want to consume. It is crucial to recognize that each household must engage in two kinds of production in order to consume. One kind is what we ordinarily think of as "work," which is intended to earn income to buy goods and services. The second kind is equally important, however, in that the effort and time of household members is required to transform goods and services purchased with household income into commodities that contribute to the household's well-being.[3] For example, much search time, maintenance time, and other time must be used to transform a building, or house, into the home or dwelling used by a household; shopping and preparation time must be combined with food and cooking equipment to produce home-cooked meals or nutrition. Seen from this point of view, retail merchants play a crucial role in helping households produce these commodities efficiently, so that they may reap the benefits of the high productivity arising from specialization in production for the market.

Imagine what it would be like if retail trade did not exist to facilitate specialization in the production of commodities for household consumption. In order to prepare a meal, one would either have to grow one's own food, arrange to barter with a neighbor, or use

[3] This terminology and approach is based on the paper by Gary S. Becker, "A Theory of the Allocation of Time," *Economics Journal*, vol. 75 (September 1965), pp. 493-517.

valuable time and other resources to find and arrange for the delivery of meat, vegetables, and fruit from a wholesale house or, worse, from producers whose farms and ranches might be located many miles away—even in foreign lands. Shopping for a suit of clothes would require finding a tailor or traveling to a distant city where a clothing factory is located. Comparison shopping might require visiting several cities instead of examining several brands in one or a few retail stores.

Retailers specialize in finding out where the goods consumers want to buy are produced at the lowest price, transporting them to convenient locations, and providing information on the range of options consumers face in allocating their incomes among alternative choices. The efficiency with which retailers perform this task is of the utmost importance in determining the standard of living we attain, given our abilities to produce goods and services for the market.

How the Retail Trade Industry Works. The retail trade industry in the United States and in most other countries is highly competitive in that competing firms quickly exploit opportunities to earn unusually high profits by providing customers with a less expensive product or a new good to use in the production of consumable commodities. Thus, on the average, firms' owners earn a return on their labor and investments just sufficient to keep them in business in the industry. Management that is unsuccessful in offering for sale those goods most desired by consumers or in providing a given quality of service and range of products at a price as low as offered by the most efficient firms will soon find that its services are no longer in demand.

We can better assess the impact of minimum wage legislation on the retail trade industry if we explore in some detail the way retail service is provided in a competitive market. Retail service consists of elements that are themselves inputs into a higher production process in which householders combine their time, goods, and the service provided by the retail trade industry to produce commodities such as shelter, nutrition, entertainment, and recreation. Retail service is a multidimensional mixture of information, transportation, credit, and convenience that is extremely difficult to describe and measure precisely. Considerable progress in understanding the industry is possible, however, if we recognize that, in a competitive environment, the typical firm's total cost of providing retail services is measured by its realized gross profit margin—that is, the value of sales less the cost of goods sold. This quantity includes a normal return to the firm's equity capital; interest on borrowed funds; the wages of management, sales personnel, office staff, and buying staff; advertising; and the transportation cost of bringing goods from manufacturers and wholesalers, as well as "free" delivery to customers. All of these costs reflect the firm's decisions on how much service to provide its customers and the least-cost way to combine purchased inputs (factors of production) to produce it. The least-cost combination of factors permits the firm to achieve the greatest possible profit from its endeavors. Under competitive conditions, however, attempts by all firms to obtain the largest possible profit result in the typical firm's operating so that retail services are produced at the lowest possible cost, while the largest possible profit is only barely large enough to keep the owners of the inputs used from selling them to firms in other industries.

Competition among firms assures that only those that succeed in providing the components of retail service demanded by consumers will survive. The type and quantities of these components demanded are determined by household decisions on which commodities to produce and how to produce them. Relatively little is known about the nature of household production because relatively few data are systematically collected on the way household members allocate their time and purchases among alternative activities, and because measuring the output of commodities such as recreation, shelter, and nutrition is conceptually difficult. Nevertheless, it is instructive to speculate on the way changes in wealth, wage rates, and knowledge may affect the quantity and type of retail service households demand, given the cost of providing it.

Better educated customers. Perhaps the most important variable influencing household production and labor force behavior over the years has been the increase in the level of schooling acquired by the typical individual. Increased schooling has influenced many aspects of economic life. Perhaps the most obvious among these is earning power.[4] A well-educated worker earns more because he or she is a more productive employee. This provides households with a greater ability to purchase goods and services from retail stores. Increased purchasing power, however, is by no means the only consequence of greater schooling. The higher wage rates responsible for rising real income levels also mean that using an individual's time in home production is more costly. Each hour that is used, say, to shop for food, prepare a meal, care for a child, or paint a house is an hour that is no longer available to trade for income in the labor market. Thus, it seems reasonable to expect higher wage rates to influence the kinds

[4] See, for example, Belton M. Fleisher and Thomas J. Kniesner, *Labor Economics: Theory, Evidence, and Policy*, 2nd ed. (Englewood Cliffs, N.J.: Prentice-Hall, 1980), pp. 342-46.

of retail services demanded by households, given the cost of these services. Because of the greater value of their time, more affluent customers will be more likely to shop in stores where service is relatively prompt and waiting time is relatively short. Shopping centers, which reduce travel time between stores and facilitate purchasing a wide variety of goods in one shopping trip, are likely to have great appeal. Products that economize on time spent in household production, such as automatic laundry equipment, frost-free refrigerators, "boil in the bag" foods, and so on, will become relatively more popular.

Increased schooling also is likely to result in more knowledgeable consumers who are more effective in the use of their time outside the labor market as well as on the job. Relatively well-educated consumers are more likely to demand products that employ high levels of technology (such as microwave ovens with elaborate operating instructions), and they are more likely to be able to evaluate the merits of alternative versions of a product by reading technical literature in trade and consumer publications as well as at the point of sale. Therefore, less-skilled sales personnel will be needed to assist in reaching a decision on which brands of which goods to purchase. Clearly, rising educational attainment bears implications for the retail industry that individual firms may ignore only at the peril of their survival in the market place.

Increasing number of married women in the labor force. Perhaps the most widely discussed change in households over the past twenty-five years has been the increasing labor force participation of married women.[5] The fact that increasing numbers of wives and mothers are working for pay has clearly altered the type of retail services demanded by a typical household, since this change has not been offset by an equal reduction in the labor force participation of husbands. An analysis of the influence of the changing role of women in society, however, reveals that the basic forces at work are the same as those discussed in the preceding section. That women are more likely to work nowadays than a generation ago implies that their time is now more valuable than before in terms of income forgone per hour spent in household activities. Moreover, their greater productivity in the labor market—helping to generate greater family wealth—has been accompanied by increasing knowledge applied to household production and concomitant changes in the demand for retail services. The impact of the growing number of wives in the labor force on the demand for retail services is akin to that of increased schooling.

[5] See ibid., pp. 125-32.

The supply of retail services. The interrelationship between retail trade and the rest of the economy is complex, and the rising levels of schooling, market wage rates, and productivity that affect the demand for retail services have also influenced the cost of supplying them. As technological advance and schooling have raised labor productivity and, hence, wage rates, the cost of employing an hour of labor in retail trade has risen along with labor cost in other industries. If technological advance in the provision of retail services proceeded at the same pace as in the rest of the economy, then the effect of rising wage rates on the cost of retail services relative to the effect on the cost of, say, manufactured goods would be nil. The increasing cost of a unit of labor would be offset by rising efficiency in its use in both industries. Suppose, however, that technological progress is greater in the goods-producing sector of the economy than in the trade and service sector. Since workers will tend to seek employment where their earning power is highest, employers in retail trade will have to pay them what they could earn in the goods-producing industries. The cost of providing retail services will tend to increase relative to the cost of goods. Thus, while on the demand side rising wage rates of consumers increase the value of their time, leading them to substitute bought labor in retail trade for their own time in household production, the rising cost of retail services induced by rising wage rates works in the opposite direction.

Retailers, facing rising costs of hired labor, will try to reduce the impact on the cost of providing retail services by substituting alternative inputs. In general, any employer facing an increase in the price of one factor relative to the price of the others will find that, in order to produce a given level and quality of output at its lowest cost, it is necessary to use fewer units of the relatively more expensive input and more of those inputs whose relative price has fallen. Thus, substitution of mechanical and electronic equipment for human inputs in retail trade has occurred in the handling of cash, credit and accounting operations, stocking shelves, and so on. This process of substitution for relatively costly labor will, through its effect of attenuating the increasing price of retail service, tend to reduce the impact of rising wage rates on the quantity of retail services demanded by consumers.

The tendency for increasing wage rates to cause the cost of retail services to rise over time may induce further input adjustments by retailers. Retailers can offset the increasing trend in labor costs, not only by substituting nonhuman inputs for labor, but also by substituting among labor categories. By using a higher proportion of younger and less well-educated workers, by employing more women and fewer men, by making efforts to break down discrimination barriers against blacks and other minority groups, retail employers can attenuate rising labor costs. In general, these substitutions among labor categories cannot be accomplished while maintaining unchanged the nature and composition of retail service. This is most obvious when younger (less experienced) or less well-educated workers are substituted for those with greater experience and schooling.

Although it may not be obvious that altering the composition of retail service is a workable means for retail firms to deal with rising labor costs, there are reasons for suspecting that it has been a profit-maximizing procedure in many instances. A numerical example will help illustrate one reason why an increase in the price of labor exerts a force toward altering the type of retail service offered to consumers. Suppose that a store can sell 1,000 units of goods per year with either of the input combinations shown in table 1. Technique A is relatively intensive in its use of trained sales personnel, whereas technique B is relatively intensive in its use of cashiers and shelf-stockers. With technique A, customers receive a great deal of personal attention, but occasionally must queue up to be waited on; with technique B, customers find it much more difficult to obtain answers to their questions about different brands or models of goods, but those who are knowledgeable about their alternatives can find what they want relatively quickly on adequately stocked, open shelves and then pay for their purchases. Technique A is relatively high quality since it uses more skilled personnel and more labor on balance than technique B.

Now, suppose that the cost of goods to a store is $80, the cost of physical equipment is $1,000 per unit per year, salespersons earn $10,000, and cashiers and shelf-stockers earn $5,000 per year. The store's total annual cost of operations is $165,000 if it adopts technique A and $140,000 if it operates with technique B. If the wages of all types of labor should double, the firm's operations would cost $240,000 with technique A, while the cost of operating with technique B would rise to $190,000. We assume that labor productivity in the goods-producing industry doubles, but that it remains

TABLE 1

INPUTS FOR ALTERNATIVE TECHNIQUES FOR PRODUCING RETAIL SERVICES

Technique	*Trained Sales Personnel*	*Cashiers and Shelf-Stockers*	*Physical Equipment*
A	6	3	10
B	1	8	10

unchanged in retail trade. This implies that the cost of a unit of goods purchased from the manufacturer does not rise. However, the technology with which sales personnel, cashiers, and stockers perform their tasks is unchanged. Since labor costs initially constitute 45 percent of the total cost of technique A (including the cost of goods sold) and only 36 percent of the cost of technique B, a doubling of the cost of labor causes a greater relative increase in the store's total costs if it operates with technique A—45.4 percent—than if it operates with technique B—35.7 percent. Consider the impact of this change in relative costs on consumers' choices. Before labor costs rose, a consumer would have to spend 17.9 percent more for a good purchased from a store using the high-quality technique A than from a store using technique B ($165.00 per good versus $140.00). After the increase in labor costs, the premium required to shop in store A is 26 percent ($240.00 versus $190.00). In other words, an equivalent rise in all labor costs results in an increase in the relative cost of high-quality versus low-quality retail services.

The basic assumptions upon which this example depends are (1) that productivity increases more rapidly in the economy's goods-producing industries than in retail trade and (2) that the share of labor in total cost is greater in high-quality retail operations than in low-quality ones. The first assumption is difficult to document because hard data measuring the output of retail personnel in terms of the services they perform (as opposed to the number of goods sold per worker) are difficult to obtain; however, casual observation appears to support the assumption. Moreover, to the extent technological advances have permitted productivity to increase in retail trade, they probably have benefited the type of operation characterized by technique B in the example rather than by technique A. Electronic data processing, for example, has greatly streamlined the coordination of sales transactions, cash and credit control, and inventory management, while improved materials handling equipment and packaging techniques have reduced the labor required to stock and display goods in self-service operations. Even without increasing labor costs, such innovations would tend to lower the relative cost of procedures that make use of less-skilled workers as opposed to knowledgeable and experienced sales personnel. The second assumption seems reasonable enough, although it too is difficult to document because available data are not typically categorized according to retail service "quality." The data in table 2, however, suggest that the assumption is valid.

Summary. On the demand side, rising wage rates induce households to substitute retail services, including the time of retail em-

TABLE 2

LABOR COST AS A PERCENTAGE OF SALES, BY KIND OF BUSINESS, 1954[a]

Kind of Business	*Percent*
Food stores	
High quality	
Meat markets	8.3
Fruit stores and vegetable markets	8.5
Direct selling (house-to-house)	19.0
Low quality	
Grocery stores	6.6
General merchandise	
High quality	
Department stores	16.8
Direct selling	30.0
Low quality	
Variety stores	16.1
Mail order houses	14.2

[a] Establishments with payroll.

SOURCE: U.S. Bureau of the Census, *Census of Business, 1954,* vol. 1, *Retail Trade—Summary Statistics* (1958), table 10.

ployees, for their own time in shopping for goods and in producing household commodities. Rising schooling and knowledge, in conjunction with increases in the value consumers place on their own time, plausibly create a bias toward those kinds of retail service that economize on shopping time and away from forms of retailing that are time-intensive for the shopper (characterized by a one-to-one relationship between sales personnel and retail customers). At the same time, rising real wage rates and affluence of consumers create a wealth effect causing the demand for retail services and retail employees to increase. More retail purchases per individual imply more retail employees per individual, other things being equal.

On the supply side, greater productivity-increases in the goods-producing sector of the economy than in retail trade causes the cost of retail service to rise relative to goods and the price of high-quality service to rise relative to low-quality. The net outcome of these opposing forces is ambiguous in principle, but on balance one would be surprised to observe an increase in the relative number of high-wage retail employees, given the mix of incentives that have worked in favor of substitution in the opposite direction.

Trends in the Quantity and Quality of Employment and Service in Distribution

The data in table 3 show how employment in the trade industries has grown over the years, relative to both the population and the total labor force. In 1960, the number of persons served by a typical worker in trade was only 42 percent of the number in 1870. Over the same period, the number of workers in the goods-producing industries divided by persons in the population industries fell by 41 percent. Between 1940 and 1970, the ratio of the U.S. population to the number of workers in retail trade fell from 26.3 to 18.5. Whatever forces existed on the cost side to reduce the number of retail trade workers "hired" by a typical consumer were evidently offset by

TABLE 3

EMPLOYMENT TRENDS IN TRADE AND THE U.S. ECONOMY, 1870–1970[a]

Year	*Employment in Trade ÷ Population*		*Employment in Wholesale and Retail Trade ÷ Labor Force*	*Employment in Goods-Producing Industries[b] ÷ Population*
	Trade	Retail trade		
1870	0.032	—	0.101	0.257
1880	0.038	—	0.111	0.267
1890	0.047	—	0.127	0.259
1900	0.052	—	0.136	0.262
1910	0.058	—	0.142	0.251
1920	0.055	—	0.140	0.230
1930	0.065	—	0.166	0.191
1940	0.071	0.038	0.166	0.180
1950	0.081	0.045	0.186	0.181
1960	0.077	0.046	0.190	0.152
1970	—	0.054	—	—

[a] The number of employees in trade reported here exceeds the total number of employees in wholesale and retail trade reported in the U.S. Census or Current Population Reports in comparable years. These, however, are the best available data for examining the trend in employment over time. See Stanley Lebergott, "Labor Force and Employment 1800–1960," in *Output, Employment, and Productivity in the United States after 1800*, Conference on Research in Income and Wealth, Studies in Income and Wealth, vol. 30 (New York: National Bureau of Economic Research, 1966).

[b] Agriculture, fishing, mining, construction, and manufacturing.

SOURCE: U.S. Bureau of the Census, *Historical Statistics of the United States, Colonial Times to 1970* (1975), Series A6, D136, D167–181.

a wealth-induced increase in purchases of retail goods and their concomitant retail services.

The tremendous increase in productivity in the goods-producing industries and the increased proportion of goods passing through retail outlets on their way to their final users has caused the number of goods processed per hour worked in retail trade to grow considerably—by about 160 percent during the eighty-year period 1869–1949, for example.[6] More recently—between 1929 and 1963—sales of goods (in constant dollars) per hour worked in retail trade grew by about 1.73 percent a year.[7] While we have no way of knowing precisely how rapidly the average quantity of retail service per consumer was growing over time, we have some indirect evidence regarding its rate of growth. It seems plausible to assume that, if the quality of the labor force in retail trade does not decline, then the quantity of retail service produced with an hour of work does not decline. Whether, with constant worker quality, retail service labor productivity rises depends on the quantity of other inputs per worker and technological progress.

The data in table 4 suggest that, over the sixty years between 1869 and 1929, the quality of labor employed in trade did not decline relative to the quality of labor employed in production industries (agriculture, mining, and manufacturing). Indeed, the opposite appears to be true, since the relative wage rate in trade rose by about 17 percent. After 1929, however, an abrupt decline began, continuing through 1961. After 1961, the relative wage in retail trade began to rise, but it has remained much below its 1929 level. The decline in relative average hourly earnings in retail trade totaled 22 percent by 1961, an average rate of decline of 1.1 percent a year. This decline is extremely important in assessing the impact of minimum wage legislation on the retail trade industry.

The period 1869–1929 was evidently one of increasing per capita consumption of the services of the trade industries. Columns (3) and (4) of table 4 show that value added as a proportion of sales grew at about 0.20 percent a year between 1869 and 1948. Between 1939 and 1977, the annual rate of growth was about 0.17 percent annually. Value added is conceptually very close to gross margin and represents payments to all inputs apart from the cost of goods sold (and transportation). Because the per capita consumption of goods clearly rose

[6] See Barger, *Distribution's Place in the American Economy*, pp. 38 and 70.

[7] David Schwartzman, "The Growth of Sales per Man-Hour in Retail Trade, 1929–1963," in Victor R. Fuchs, ed., *Production and Productivity in the Service Industries* (New York: National Bureau of Economic Research, 1969), p. 204.

TABLE 4

RELATIVE WAGE RATES AND VALUE ADDED IN TRADE, 1869–1977

Year	*Average Hourly Earnings in Trade ÷ Average Hourly Earnings in Production*[a] (1)	*Average Hourly Earnings of Nonsupervisory Workers in Retail Trade ÷ Average Hourly Earnings of Nonsupervisory Workers in Manufacturing*[b] (2)	*Value Added in Distribution ÷ Sales*[c] *(1869 = 100)* (3)	*Value Added in Wholesale and Retail Trade ÷ Retail Sales* (4)
1869	1.18	—	100	—
1879	1.41	—	103	—
1889	1.36	—	106	—
1899	1.37	—	108	—
1909	1.24	—	112	—
1919	1.25	—	112	—
1929	1.39	0.99	113	—
1939	1.18	0.77	115	0.30
1949	—	0.74	(1947) 115	(1948) 0.31
1959	—	0.72	—	(1958) 0.29
1961	—	0.72	—	(1963) 0.31
1967	—	0.77	—	0.31
1977	—	0.74	—	0.32

[a] Production is defined as agriculture, mining, and manufacturing; retail trade excludes workers in eating and drinking establishments.

[b] See appendix B for method used in deriving this series.

[c] The 1969 ratio is 0.327.

SOURCES: (1) Harold Barger, *Distribution's Place in the American Economy since 1869* (Princeton, N.J.: Princeton University Press, 1955), p. 109. (2) U.S. Department of Commerce, *U.S. National Income and Product Accounts;* U.S. Department of Labor, *Employment and Earnings,* Bulletin 1312-10. (3) Barger, *Distribution's Place in the American Economy,* p. 92. (4) U.S. Bureau of the Census, *Historical Statistics of the United States, Colonial Times to 1970* (1975), Series T1, T2, and T81; U.S. Bureau of the Census, *Statistical Abstract of the United States,* (1979), tables 1460 and 1462.

over the entire period, it follows that, if more was spent on retail services per good sold, then individual consumers were spending considerably more on distributive services in 1977 than in 1869 and, unless productivity fell substantially, they were purchasing a much greater quantity of retail service at the end of the period than at the beginning.

The net outcome of the forces of demand and supply caused the consumption of distributive services to grow more rapidly between 1869 and 1977 than the consumption of goods, but the differential rate of growth was about half again as large through 1899 as it was after the turn of the century. One suspects that an important cause was the rate of increase in specialization of tasks. One bit of evidence supporting this explanation is that the proportion of output sold to consumers through retail stores grew from 71 percent in 1869 to 80 percent in 1899, but had risen only to 81 percent by 1929.[8] It is plausible that initially the increasing complexity of consumption activities led to demand for more and better retail services per good consumed; eventually, however, the rising relative price of retail services, increasing sophistication of consumers, and a deceleration of specialization in economic functions caused this trend to slow down.

8 Barger, *Distribution's Place in the American Economy*, p. 70.

2

The Impact of Federal Minimum Wage Legislation on the Cost of Labor in Retail Trade

Theoretical Considerations

All of the effects of minimum wage legislation on own- and other-industry employment and on the distribution of wage rates and earnings arise from the simple fact that an effective wage floor increases the amount paid to those who would otherwise receive less. Production costs are raised, resulting in increased selling prices and reductions in output. Within the firm, the employment of low-productivity labor becomes less attractive relative to nonhuman inputs and higher-skilled labor. Thus, it is natural in studies of the effects of minimum wage legislation to relate all observed impacts to a measure of the increased labor cost attributable to the minimum wage.

Difficulties in Measuring the Impact of a Minimum Wage Rate. At first, calculating increased labor cost may appear to be simple. If all of a firm's employees received the same wage rate, the proportionate increase in the wage bill attributable to an effective minimum wage would be simply the ratio $(M/W) - 1$, where M is the minimum wage rate, and W is the wage rate the firm paid before the minimum became effective. Although a few industries are characterized by labor forces composed of a high proportion of homogeneous workers receiving nearly identical wage rates, employment in retail trade consists of workers diverse in their skills, training, experience, and rates of pay. In the absence of continuous data on wage rates and employment by finely divided worker-skill classes, we are required to measure the effect of a minimum wage on the average labor cost of a heterogeneous labor force receiving diverse rates of pay. When data are available on the distribution of wage rates across covered workers at some date before a minimum wage is imposed, one can calculate the change in the mean that would result if everyone currently receiving less than the minimum (corrected for the degree of wage growth to the minimum's effective date) were to receive the minimum wage. Unfortunately, the closer the observation point is to the date the minimum wage becomes effective, the greater is the probability that employers, anticipating its impact, have already substituted against low-productivity workers with higher-skilled labor. Thus, the impact of an effective minimum wage on labor cost may easily be underestimated if calculations are based on a naive use of the wage distribution.

The likelihood that substitution against low-productivity workers leads to an underestimate of the impact of minimum wage legislation on average labor cost diminishes as the time between the date when the wage frequency distribution is observed and the date when the minimum becomes effective increases. Unfortunately, the longer time period also increases the need, and difficulty, of forecasting changes in the wage distribution that would have occurred even in the absence of minimum wage legislation.

Overestimating or underestimating the effect of minimum wage rates on firms' labor costs would not be a terribly serious problem for arriving at qualitative, or even quantitative, estimates of their ultimate economic impact if the degree of error were the same over time for all firms or industries examined under the same conditions. Unfortunately, the magnitude of measurement error is likely to vary across industries, or branches of retail trade, in the same direction as the opportunities to substitute relatively cheaper for relatively more expensive inputs.

Measuring the Impact of Subsequent Increases in the Minimum Wage. The measurement difficulties discussed above arise when information is available on the frequency distribution of wage rates before the first effective date of minimum wage legislation. Further—and perhaps more serious—difficulties arise when we want to examine the effects of subsequent increases in minimum wage rates. In this case, we want to know how the minimum raises the amount paid to the average employee compared with the amount that would have been paid in the absence of minimum wage legislation. Unfortunately, it is only possible to observe the distribution of wage rates in the presence of a preexisting minimum wage rate. Thus, we again face the problem that the number of workers earning the lowest wage rates is reduced by substitution against low-productivity employees. Moreover, it is difficult to know how many of these low-paid workers would have been employed (and at what wage) had their wages and employment opportunities been determined in an unregulated labor market.

A tentative solution to the problem that employees earning less than the minimum wage are not directly observable would be to fit a statistical distribution function to the frequency distribution of wage rates observed some time before a minimum wage rate was imposed, and then use this information to infer what minimum wage recipients would have earned subsequently in a freely functioning labor market. Although such data are available and are used to help calculate the cost of paying the workers at least the minimum wage, two difficulties arise when attempting to use this procedure. First, the distribution of wage rates above the minimum will be affected by substitution toward relatively highly skilled or more experienced workers; this shift will increase the hypothetical, unregulated wage rates imputed to minimum wage recipients and thus induce an underestimate of the impact of the minimum on labor cost. Second, economic events other than minimum wage legislation occurring after the initial imposition of the minimum may cause the distribution of unregulated wage rates to rise or fall.

In the case of retail trade, for example, had there continued to be no federal minimum wage after 1961, extension of coverage in the remainder of the economy and changes in the relative level of the minimum applicable to other industries might have affected retail trade wage rates of persons seeking employment in the noncovered sector. Moreover, as noted above, there is evidence that the quality of labor employed in retail trade was declining relative to that in the goods-producing industries during the thirty years before the imposition of federal minimum wage legislation in 1961. Since the retail trade industry is a relatively important source of jobs for young workers, shifts in the proportion of young persons in the population would be expected to result in changes (in the opposite direction) of the "free market" wage in retail trade. To the extent such forces were operating, then the effect of prior minimum wage legislation seriously clouds a picture of what the distribution of wage rates would have looked like in the absence of a legislated minimum. Truncating the observed frequency distribution of wage rates at the new minimum wage will provide a measure of the incremental labor cost of increasing the legal wage floor. The total impact, however, of minimum wage legislation cannot be inferred simply from adjusting an estimate of the impact of the prior minimum downward in accordance with the average economy-wide rate of growth of wages and adding this adjusted effect of the old minimum to the estimated incremental cost. A more sophisticated technique is required to estimate the hypothetical course of wages in the covered industry had no minimum wage been enforced there. The technique used in this study to forecast the hypothetical path of the average wage in retail trade had minimum wage legislation not been extended to the industry is described below. The hypothetical forecast wage is combined with information on the distribution of wage rates to develop a measure of the impact of minimum wage rates on labor cost.

The Problem of Partial Coverage. The preceding discussion outlines several problems that arise in measuring the additional labor cost imposed on firms that are legally required to pay a minimum wage in excess of the wage that would prevail as the result of supply and demand in an unregulated labor market. An additional and equally serious problem arises because not all retail firms or establishments are subject to federal minimum wage legislation, and the proportion of employees in covered establishments has changed a great deal over time. In retail trade, minimum wage coverage has never been complete. Before 1961, only 3 percent of all retail employees were covered by federal wage and hours regulations, although 25 percent of the experienced labor force in retail trade in 1960 resided in states with legal minimum wage rates of $1.00 or more (see table 5). During the first six years of significant federal coverage (1961–1966) only one-third of nonsupervisory retail trade employees were covered, and the proportion of covered workers did not exceed two-thirds until 1976. As table 5 shows, state coverage exceeded federal coverage in the Northeast and West regions in 1960. Since then, federal legislation has been dominant, except in the Northeast region and problably in the West through 1966.

If employment and wage data were widely available for covered and noncovered workers separately over a large number of years and geographical areas, then one could study covered retail trade as a separate industry. Unfortunately, this is not the case, and the researcher must frequently use data that do not permit a distinction between workers subject to minimum wage legislation and those who are not.

The following example illustrates the significance of this problem. Suppose that it was desired to test the hypothesis that minimum wage rates reduce employment. A common method of doing this is to correlate industry employment and a measure of the impact of minimum wages on labor cost over time, using annual or quarterly data. Since direct measures of the minimum wage impact on labor cost (even flawed measures such as some of those discussed previously) are generally unavailable on an annual or quarterly basis, a proxy must be used; for instance, $M_t/\overline{W}_t$ where M is the minimum wage, $\overline{W}$ is the industry mean wage, and t is a time index. The specific

TABLE 5

Workers in Retail Trade Covered by Federal and State Minimum Wage Laws, 1960–1978

Year	Fraction of Nonsupervisory Workers Covered by Federal Legislation (percent)	Minimum Wage for Workers Covered by 1961 Federal Legislation[a] (dollars)	Fraction of Experienced Retail Trade Workers in States with Legal Minimum Wages in Retail Trade[b] (percent)					State Minimum Wage Equal to or Greater Than: (dollars)
			Total United States	Northeast	North Central	South	West	
1960	3[c]	1.00[c]	25	78	0	0	36	1.00
1961	33	1.00						
1966	33	1.25	27	75	8	1	37	1.25
1967–1968	49	1.40						
1969	58	1.60						
1970	59	1.60						

1971	60	1.60
1972	62	1.60
1973	65	1.60
1974	63	2.00
1975	66	2.10
1976	72	2.30
1977	78	2.30
1978	82	2.65

[a] For a more detailed description of coverage and minimum wage rate in retail trade, see appendix table E1.

[b] 1960 labor force data.

[c] Workers covered by 1937 legislation.

SOURCES: For federal legislation: unpublished data from the U.S. Department of Labor, Employment Standards Administration. For state legislation: U.S. Congress, House of Representatives, Subcommittee on Labor Standards of the Committee on Education and Labor, *Hearings on Various Bills Regarding Minimum Wage Legislation*, 86th Congress, 2nd session, March 16–April 13, 1960, p. 67; U.S. Bureau of the Census, *U.S. Census of Population: 1960* (1964), vol. 1, part 1, table 259, and state volumes, table 126; U.S. Department of Labor, Wage and Hour and Public Contracts Divisions, *Retail Trade: A Study to Measure the Effects of Minimum Wage and Maximum Hours Standards of the Fair Labor Standards Act* (1967), pp. 10–16.

form of the proxy makes no difference to this example.

The problem with this procedure is that, when the covered retail firms and establishments are required to increase the wage they pay to some of their employees, they have an incentive to reduce their employment of subminimum wage workers. Some of these discharged employees may leave the labor force, while others may enter the pool of unemployed workers; some, however, may obtain jobs with firms or establishments not required to pay the minimum wage. In the extreme case, all of the discharged workers obtain employment in the noncovered sector. In this situation, for retail trade in the aggregate there is no change in employment, although there is a decline in the wage rate paid to noncovered employees offsetting the increase paid to workers in the covered sector who now receive the minimum wage. If only industry-wide aggregate data are available, there will appear to be no disemployment resulting from the increase in the minimum wage. Moreover, the mean wage for the covered and noncovered sectors taken together may be unchanged, even though the proxy measure indicates an increase in industry labor cost.[1] In these circumstances, careless use of industry aggregate data will mask important effects of a minimum wage rate on employment and the distribution of earning power and may lead incorrectly to the conclusion that there is no impact.

Aggregate industry data may mask the effect of a minimum wage not only on average labor cost but also on employment. The degree by which total industry employment falls in response to the imposition of a minimum wage is opposite in sign and magnitude to the movement of the wage paid in the noncovered sector. Thus, an attempt to measure the disemployment effect of a minimum wage in an industry might be completely frustrated if only aggregate data are available, since the minimum wage may result in a shift in employment from covered to noncovered firms or establishments within the industry and a decline in the relative wage of the noncovered sector, but little or no change in aggregate employment or the industry average wage. These are important consequences of minimum wage legislation and are well worth the attention of policy makers, but they are not those predicted by a naive application of the standard labor market analysis of the impact of a minimum wage rate on all workers in a market.[2]

[1] See Finis Welch, "Minimum Wage Legislation in the United States," in Orley Ashenfelter and James Blum, eds., *Evaluating the Labor Market Effects of Social Programs* (Princeton, N.J.: Princeton University Industrial Relations Section, 1977), pp. 14-23.

[2] See appendix A for a more rigorous discussion of this problem.

Measuring the Effect of Minimum Wages on the Cost of Labor in Retail Trade

The discussion in chapter 1 of trends in employment and output of the distributive sector was intended to provide background information supporting an estimate of the impact of minimum wage legislation on the cost of labor in the retail trade industry. It was emphasized there and in the preceding section that such an estimate requires knowledge of what would have happened to wage rates in retail trade in the absence of such legislation. The best available evidence suggests that simply to extrapolate the average wage rate in retail trade on the basis of the relationship between that rate as it stood on the eve of federal legislation in early 1961 and wages in other sectors of the economy would be woefully incorrect and would lead to a substantial underestimate of the impact of minimum wage legislation on wage costs, at least in the covered sector of the industry, and hence on employment and the provision of retail services.

Earlier it was argued that the quality of labor employed in retail trade was declining before the advent of federal minimum wage regulation in the industry for at least two reasons: first, greater productivity growth in the goods-producing sector of the economy tended to increase the cost of labor in retail trade per unit of retail service; and second, increasing education and knowledge caused the typical consumer to reduce the demand for relatively skilled, experienced, and knowledgeable sales personnel in an increasing proportion of retail transactions.

Moreover, minimum wage legislation itself may have acted as a force to lower the average wage of workers in retail trade relative to the rest of the economy. By reducing employment opportunities for low-wage workers in covered firms after 1938, the Fair Labor Standards Act (FLSA) is likely to have resulted in a shift of these workers toward noncovered firms. Table 6 shows how FLSA coverage varied across industry groups and over time from 1938 to 1978. Since coverage was negligible in retail trade until September 1961, employment of low-wage workers could be expected to have grown more rapidly in retail trade than in other industries, even if the conditions discussed above were not working in the same direction.

Changing Characteristics of the Retail Trade Labor Force. The wage data in table 4 show that a decline in the relative average hourly earnings of workers in retail trade began in the late 1920s or early 1930s and continued through the 1950s. This decline was largely attributable

TABLE 6

PROPORTION OF NONSUPERVISORY EMPLOYEES COVERED BY THE FAIR LABOR STANDARDS ACT, 1938–1978
(percent)

Year	*Retail Trade*	*Manufacturing*	*Nonfarm Industries outside Retail Trade*
1938	3	67	34
1947	3	95	75
1961	33	96	76
1967	49	97	83
1970	59	97	84
1975	66	97	88
1978	82	97	90

SOURCE: Unpublished data of the U.S. Department of Labor, Employment Standards Administration, and various issues of U.S. Department of Labor, Bureau of Labor Statistics, *Employment and Earnings.*

to a greater proportion of workers who typically receive relatively low wage rates because of their age, experience, race, or sex, as opposed to a decline in the wages paid to workers of given characteristics, and it is consistent with the quality hypothesis suggested above. Data showing some of these changes in the relative age, sex, and racial composition of the retail trade labor force are presented in tables 7 through 10. Between 1930 and 1950, the proportion of relatively low-paid workers (teenagers, women, blacks) was growing more rapidly in retail trade than in the rest of the economy. Between 1950 and 1960, the proportion of teenagers and blacks continued to grow more rapidly in retail trade, but the trend reversed in the case of female relative to male workers.

In the period following 1960, the relatively more rapid substitution of black workers for white and of teenage workers for adult in retail trade reversed itself or slowed down sharply. These disruptions in the trend toward increasing employment of low-wage workers are probably attributable to the imposition of federal minimum wage regulation in retail trade.

David Schwartzman has also noted the importance of the changing characteristics of the retail trade labor force.[3] Based on 1960 earnings differentials among workers categorized according to their age, sex, and education, Schwartzman estimated that changes in the mix of these characteristics among members of the U.S. labor force

[3] David Schwartzman, "The Growth of Sales per Man-Hour in Retail Trade, 1929–1963," in Victor R. Fuchs, ed., *Production and Productivity in the Service Industries* (New York: National Bureau of Economic Research, 1969).

raised average earning power by 10.4 percent between 1929 and 1963. If the age-sex-education mix of the retail trade labor force relative to other industries had been the same in 1963 as in 1929, then the average wage in retail trade would have grown at the same rate as in other industries, except perhaps for short-run fluctuations associated with the business cycle. The average wage rate did not, however, grow as fast after 1930 as wage rates elsewhere. Schwartzman reports that an index of relative average hourly earnings in retail trade stood at only 73 in 1963, compared to 100 in 1929. If the index stood at 100 in both years, it could be concluded that the age, sex, and educational characteristics of retail trade workers had "grown" by 10.4 percent, just as in the rest of the economy. Schwartzman concludes that in 1963 an index of the characteristics mix of the retail trade labor force stood at $73/100 \times 110.4 = 80.6$, almost 20 percent lower than in 1929.[4]

Other Forces. In addition to differential productivity growth and growing consumer skills, other forces that may have influenced retail wages relative to the rest of the economy were no doubt at work throughout this period. One conceivably important force was differential growth in union membership among U.S. industries. Between 1929 and 1939, union membership as a proportion of the labor force did grow at a much slower rate in trade than in the rest of the economy. It is unlikely, however, that differential union growth accounts for a major portion of the decline in the relative wage of retail workers. We can estimate the impact of unionism as follows. First, we use H.G. Lewis's high estimates of the impact of unionism on the wage rates of union labor relative to nonunion labor (20 percent in 1923–1929 and in 1939–1941).[5] Second, we assume that union membership in retail trade was negligible in both 1929 and 1939.[6] Then, the decline in the wage of workers in retail trade relative to workers in manufacturing attributable to unionism would have been less than 3 percent.[7] Of course, part of the influence of unions on

---

[4] Ibid.

[5] H.G. Lewis, *Unionism and Relative Wages in the United States* (Chicago: University of Chicago Press, 1963), p. 193.

[6] No data are available for 1939. Union membership was 0.6 percent of persons engaged in wholesale and retail trade in 1929 and 9.1 percent in 1953. Union membership in trade, finance, and services grew from 1.3 percent in 1929 to 4.2 percent in 1939. See Lewis, *Unionism and Relative Wages*, p. 250.

[7] Let the wage rate of workers in manufacturing relative to workers in retail trade in the absence of unions equal 1. Then, in 1929 the relative wage in the presence of existing union membership would be the product of the impact of unions on relative wage rates and the proportion of workers who are union members, or $0.2 \times 0.083 + 1$. In 1939, the figure would be $0.2 \times 0.228 + 1$. Thus $(1 + 0.2 \times 0.083)/(1 + 0.2 \times 0.228) = 0.972$.

TABLE 7

RELATIVE YOUTH INTENSITY OF THE U.S. LABOR FORCE IN WHOLESALE AND RETAIL TRADE, 1930–1978

	Employed Teenagers (14–19) Relative to All Other Employed Persons[a]				*Employed Wage and Salary Workers 16–19 Years Old Relative to All Other Employed Wage and Salary Workers*				
Year	U.S. labor force (1)	Wholesale and retail trade (2)	*Column (2) ÷ Column (1)* (3)	*Proportionate Change in Column (2) Less Proportionate Change in Column (1)* (4)	U.S. labor force (5)	Retail trade except eating and drinking places (6)	*Column (6) ÷ Column (5)* (7)	*Proportionate Change in Column (6) Less Proportionate Change in Column (5)* (8)	*Number of Persons in U.S. Population Age 16–19 ÷ Number of Persons Age 20 and Over* (9)
1930	0.101	0.0965	0.956						0.123
1940	0.0627	0.0638	1.02	0.040	0.0603	0.0897	1.48		0.115

1950	0.0638	0.0853	1.34	0.319	0.0606	0.120	1.98	0.333	0.085
1960					0.0656	0.161	2.45	0.259	0.095
1970					0.0804	0.206	2.56	0.054	0.119
1978					0.0894	0.218	2.44	—0.10	0.117

[a] See qualifying note to table 3 in the Welch paper cited below.

SOURCES: Columns (1)–(8): 1930 and 1940, for columns (1) and (2), Finis Welch, "Minimum Wage Legislation in the United States," in Orley Ashenfelter and James Blum, eds., *Evaluating the Labor Market Effects of Social Programs* (Princeton, N.J.: Princeton University Industrial Relations Section, 1977), p. 16; 1940, for columns (4) and (5), U.S. Bureau of the Census, *Census of Population: 1940*, vol. III, *The Labor Force*, part 2, *Occupational and Industrial Characteristics*, table 3; 1950, *Census of Population: 1950*, vol. IV, *Special Reports*, P-E No. 1-D, *Industrial Characteristics*, table 4; 1960, *Census of Population: 1960*, vol. II *Subject Reports*, PC(2)-7F, *Industrial Characteristics*, table 5; 1970, *Census of Population: 1970*, 1:100 public use sample; 1978, *Current Population Survey, March 1978*, public use sample. Column (9): 1930 and 1950, *U.S. Census of Population: 1950*, vol. II, *Characteristics of the Population*, part 1, *U.S. Summary*, table 38; 1940, *U.S. Census of Population: 1940*, vol. IV, *Population*, part 1, table 1; 1960, *U.S. Census of Population: 1960*, vol. 1, *Characteristics of the Population*, part 1, *U.S. Summary*, tables 46, 47; 1970, *U.S. Census of Population: 1970*, vol. 1, *Characteristics of the Population*, part 1, *U.S. Summary*, section 1, tables 50, 52; 1978, *Current Population Survey, March 1978*, public use sample.

TABLE 8

RELATIVE FEMALE INTENSITY OF THE U.S. LABOR FORCE IN WHOLESALE AND RETAIL TRADE, 1930–1978

(number of women relative to number of men)

	Experienced Civilian Labor Force			*Employed Wage and Salary Workers*		
Year	U.S. labor force (1)	Wholesale and retail trade (2)	Proportionate change in column (2) less proportionate change in column (1) (3)	U.S. labor force (4)	Retail trade except eating and drinking places (5)	Proportionate change in column (5) less proportionate change in column (4) (6)
1930[a]	0.282	0.274				
1940[b]	0.323	0.372	0.210	0.404	0.421	
1950[b]	0.392	0.516	0.176	0.461	0.597	0.275
1960[b]				0.539	0.662	−0.059
1970[c]				0.649	0.789	−0.0116
1978[c]				0.740	0.847	−0.068

[a] Age 10 and over.

[b] Age 14 and over.

[c] Age 16 and over.

SOURCES: 1930, U.S. Bureau of the Census, *Census of Population: 1930*, vol. V, *General Report of Occupations*, chapter 7, "Gainful Workers by Industry and Occupation," table 1; 1940, *Census of Population: 1940*, vol. III, *The Labor Force*, part 1, *U.S. Summary*, table 78; 1950, *Census of Population: 1950*, vol. IV, *Special Reports*, P-E No. 1-D, *Industrial Characteristics*, tables 2, 12; 1960, *Census of Population: 1960*, vol. II, *Subject Reports*, PC(2)-7F, *Industrial Characteristics*, tables 1, 2, 3, 5 (Negro), 7; 1970, *Census of Population: 1970*, vol. II, *Subject Reports*, Final Report PC(2)-7B, *Industrial Characteristics*, tables 1, 2, 32, 33, 37, 38; 1978, *Current Population Survey, March 1978*, public use sample.

relative wages would operate through a shift of low-productivity workers from the unionized sector of the economy to the nonunionized sector as employers adjusted to a new set of relative factor prices. Moreover, the impact of unions on relative wage rates cannot be viewed as independent of the influence of federal minimum wage legislation. By restricting the ability of nonunionized firms to compete effectively against their unionized counterparts, minimum wage legislation increases the power of unions to raise the wage rates of their members relative to workers who are neither union members nor employees in firms required to observe legal wage floors.

TABLE 9

RATIO OF WOMEN TO TEENAGERS (16–19 YEARS OLD) IN THE U.S. LABOR FORCE AND IN WHOLESALE AND RETAIL TRADE, 1930–1978[a]

	Experienced Civilian Labor Force			Employed Wage and Salary Workers		
Year	U.S. labor force (1)	Wholesale and retail trade (2)	Proportionate change in column (2) less proportionate change in column (1) (3)	U.S. labor force (4)	Retail trade except eating and drinking places (5)	Proportionate change in column (5) less proportionate change in column (4) (6)
1930	1.673	1.601				
1940	2.916	3.015	0.140	3.538	2.378	
1950				4.187	2.506	−0.130
1960				4.587	2.275	−0.188
1970				4.078	1.916	−0.047
1978				3.867	1.676	−0.073

[a] The ratio of 10-15 year year olds to 10-19 year olds in retail trade is assumed to equal that in the total labor force of "gainful workers" (14.2 percent).

SOURCES: Same as table 7 except: 1930, chapter 4, "Age of Gainful Workers"; 1940, *The Labor Force* (Sample Statistics), part 2, *Occupational and Industrial Characteristics*, table 3; 1950, table 4; 1960, table 5; 1970, 1:100 public use sample.

Forecasting the Course of Wage Rates in Retail Trade after 1961. Appendix B contains a detailed statistical analysis of the method and procedures used to estimate the impact of minimum wage legislation on the average cost of labor in the retail trade industry. The results of that analysis are summarized here. Briefly, it was found that three variables—the proportion of young persons (ages fifteen to twenty-four) in the population, the proportion of military personnel in the population, and the proportionate effect of minimum wage rates outside the retail trade industry—can account for over three-quarters of the variation in the ratio of the average wage rate in retail trade to that in durable goods manufacturing. It is assumed that, if these three explanatory variables remained constant, then inflation- and productivity-caused increases in wage rates would be the same in both durable goods manufacturing and retail trade. Moreover, since employees in durable goods manufacturing earn relatively high wage rates, they are only minimally affected by federal minimum wage

TABLE 10

THE NUMBER OF BLACKS RELATIVE TO WHITES IN THE U.S. LABOR FORCE AND IN WHOLESALE AND RETAIL TRADE, 1930–1978

	Experienced Civilian Labor Force			*Employed Persons*			*Employed Wage and Salary Workers*		
Year	U.S labor force (1)	Wholesale and retail trade (2)	Proportionate change in column (2) less proportionate change in column (1) (3)	U.S. labor force (4)	Retail trade except eating and drinking places (5)	Proportionate change in column (5) less proportionate change in column (4) (6)	U.S. labor force (7)	Retail trade except eating and drinking places (8)	Proportionate change in column (8) less proportionate change in column (7) (9)
1930[a]	0.127	0.036							
1940[b]	0.096	0.058	0.842	0.095	0.050				
1950[b]				0.107	0.050	−0.134	0.111	0.058	
1960[b]				0.104	0.057	0.161	0.113	0.066	0.111
1970[c]				0.107	0.066	0.133	0.113	0.071	0.069
1978							0.110	0.066	−0.041

[a] Age 10 and over.
[b] Age 14 and over.
[c] Age 16 and over.
SOURCES: See table 7.

legislation. In other words, durable goods manufacturing appears to be a good benchmark for predicting changes in retail trade wage rates.

The relationship between the retail–durable goods manufacturing wage ratio and the three explanatory variables was estimated over the period 1936–1961, which encompasses the period beginning two years before the effective date of federal minimum wage legislation and ends three months after the effective date of federal minimum wage legislation in retail trade. Then, assuming that this relationship would have held over the next sixteen years if minimum wage legislation had not been imposed on the retail trade industry, it was used to forecast the course that retail wage rates would have taken under those circumstances.

This hypothetical time path of retail wage rates is depicted in figure 1 as the series W_{rt}^*. Evidently, the downward trend in retail trade wage rates relative to the wage rates in the goods-producing industries discussed at length above would have continued into the 1970s had minimum wage legislation not prevented continuation of the trend. Based on what I have chosen as the best forecast of retail trade wage rates from 1962 through 1978 (table B2, row 4), the ratio of wages in retail trade to those in durable goods manufacturing would have fallen about 8 percent between 1960 and 1961. This downward trend would have reversed itself around 1969; as late as 1977, however, the forecast wage ratio would still have been over 2 percent less than in 1961. By contrast the observed wage ratio actually rose slightly, reaching a peak in 1970, then declining, but in 1977 still remaining above its 1961 value. The observed retail trade wage rate is shown as series W_{rt} in figure 1.

The proportionate difference between the observed and forecast wage rates $(W_{rt} - W_{rt}^*) \div W_{rt}^*$ is also shown in figure 1, as well as in table 11. It reaches its peak during the period 1968–1970. One reason why the forecast wage rate falls below the observed wage rate by so much during the late 1960s and early 1970s can be seen in table B5. The proportion of persons aged fifteen to twenty-four in the population—the "baby boom" cohort entering the labor market—reached its peak during these years. Minimum wage rates in retail trade prevented this increase in the supply of inexperienced workers from reducing the average wage as much as would have occurred if there had been no federally mandated wage floor.

Employment opportunities for these young workers were reduced as well, as is discussed in chapter 3. Table 7 shows that the ratio of teenagers to all other employed wage and salary workers grew much more rapidly in retail trade than in other industries through 1960—at least in part, presumably, because of the disemployment effects of

FIGURE 1
FORECAST AND OBSERVED VALUES OF THE AVERAGE WAGE RATE AND ALTERNATIVE MEASURES OF MINIMUM WAGE IMPACT ON AVERAGE HOURLY EARNINGS IN RETAIL TRADE, 1962–1978

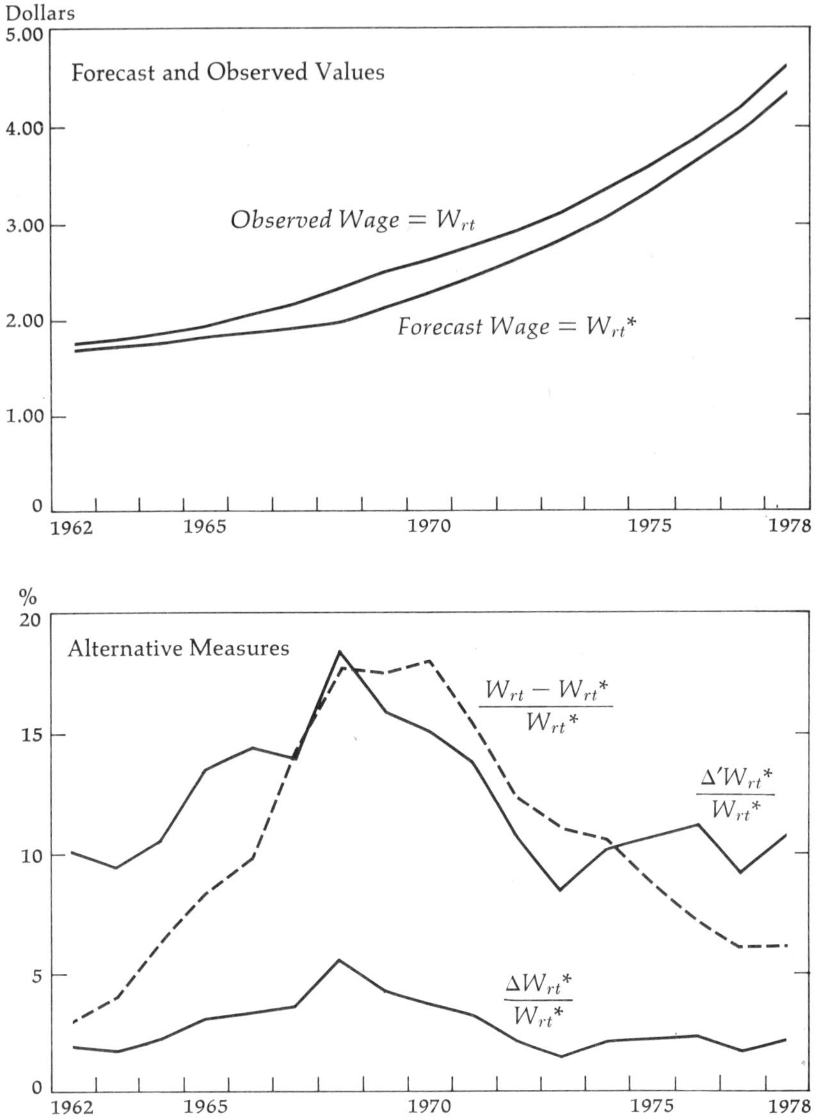

SOURCES: For forecast and observed values, table B3; for alternative measures, table 11.

TABLE 11

ALTERNATIVE MEASURES OF THE PROPORTIONATE INCREASE IN AVERAGE HOURLY EARNINGS IN COVERED RETAIL TRADE ESTABLISHMENTS RESULTING FROM FEDERAL MINIMUM WAGE LEGISLATION, 1961–1978

Year	$\frac{\Delta W_{rt}^*}{W_{rt}^*}$ (1)	$\frac{\Delta' W_{rt}^*}{W_{rt}^*}$ (2)	$\frac{\Delta' W_{rt}^*}{W_{rt}^*}$ × *Coverage Rate* (3)	$\frac{W_{rt} - W_{rt}^*}{W_{rt}^*}$ (4)	*U.S. Department of Labor*[a] Estimate (5)	Effective date[b]	Survey date[c]
1961	0.007	0.081	0.024	0.006	0.009	9/61	6/61
1962	0.020	0.101	0.030	0.030			
1963	0.018	0.094	0.029	0.040			
1964	0.022	0.105	0.028	0.063			
1965	0.031	0.135	0.039	0.083	0.006	9/65	6/65
1966	0.034	0.144	0.038	0.097			
1967	0.036	0.141	0.058	0.142	0.014	2/67	6/66
1968	0.055	0.184	0.071	0.177			
1969	0.042	0.160	0.081	0.175			
1970	0.037	0.151	0.076	0.179			
1971	0.032	0.139	0.074	0.154			
1972	0.021	0.107	0.061	0.122			
1973	0.015	0.084	0.050	0.110			
1974	0.021	0.102	0.062	0.105			
1975	0.022	0.107	0.065	0.086			
1976	0.023	0.111	0.074	0.071			
1977	0.017	0.091	0.068	0.061			
1978	0.021	0.106	0.081	0.062			

[a] Does not include newly covered establishments.
[b] Effective date of minimum wage.
[c] Date of wage survey used for estimate.

SOURCES: Columns (1)–(3), see text. Column (4), U.S. Department of Labor, Wage and Hour and Public Contracts Divisions, *Retail Trade: A Study of the Effects of the 1961 Amendments* (1967), tables 2, 5, or *Retail Trade: An Interim Study of the Effects of the 1961 Amendments* (1966), tables 7, A-2.

minimum wage legislation outside retail trade. In the decade of the 1960s, however, when retail trade first experienced federal minimum wage legislation, the rate of increase in the ratio of teenage workers to those age twenty and over increased only slightly more rapidly in retail trade than in the other industries. Between 1970 and 1978, the ratio increased less rapidly in retail trade than elsewhere.

The Impact of the Minimum Wage on the Cost of Labor in Retail Trade. It is tempting to use the difference between the observed and forecast wage rates, $W_{rt} - W_{rt}^*$, as a measure of the increased cost per hour of labor attributable to minimum wage legislation, since the minimum wage is presumably the only systematic influence on retail trade wages not represented in the relationship on which the forecast wage is based. As was pointed out, however, $W_{rt} - W_{rt}^*$ reflects a number of responses to the imposition of a minimum wage, only one of which involves raising the rate of pay of covered workers earning less than the legal minimum to that level. Since we desire a measure of increased labor cost against which to compare adjustments in labor inputs, it is better to devise a measure that is not itself dependent on those adjustments, although $W_{rt} - W_{rt}^*$ is certainly of interest as one summary measure of the effects of minimum wage legislation.

Two important adjustments of labor inputs in response to the imposition of a minimum wage will tend to increase $W_{rt} - W_{rt}^*$. One of these adjustments is the so-called ripple effect that results when firms shift their demand away from low-productivity workers who had been paid less than the minimum toward workers with greater skills, training, ability, and experience.[8] This shift will tend to raise the wages of workers above the minimum and increase their relative importance in the mix of retail trade employees, thus raising the observed mean wage rate. As Finis Welch points out, the shift toward an increasing proportion of high-wage workers in part offsets the increased cost of paying low-wage workers the minimum wage, because the former are more productive workers than those who had been paid less than the minimum.[9] To this extent, $W_{rt} - W_{rt}^*$ tends to overstate the impact of the minimum on labor cost correctly measured. The second adjustment affecting the observed mean wage is similar to the first. It occurs when, instead of simply raising all subminimum workers to the minimum wage, firms discharge all or part of this class of employees. Again, the proportion of high-wage workers is increased—raising the mean wage to an extent determined by the shape of the demand curve for low-wage employees. Paradoxically, this impact on $W_{rt} - W_{rt}^*$ will be greater the easier it is for firms to do without low-wage labor. If firms find relatively high-wage workers a good substitute for low-wage employees (because they are so much more useful), then the ultimate impact of a minimum wage on the cost of retail service is relatively small, although there is a large decline in the employment of low-wage workers.

[8] See Finis Welch, *Minimum Wages: Issues and Evidence* (Washington, D.C.: American Enterprise Institute, 1978), pp. 26-28.
[9] Ibid.

A measure of increased labor cost that is not influenced by firms' adjustments to the minimum wage is the proportionate increase in the forecast wage required to bring all workers to at least the minimum wage, $\Delta W_{rt}^*/W_{rt}^*$. It is devoid of the problems described in the preceding paragraph, and it can be compared with similar measures used by the Department of Labor, based on the observed wage distribution. Calculation of $\Delta W_{rt}^*/W_{rt}^*$ is made possible by the existence of data on the distribution of wage rates among retail trade workers published by the U.S. Department of Labor in 1956 (see appendix B for details). By assuming that this distribution would have remained approximately unchanged over the years, except for increases in the forecast retail trade mean wage rate, if minimum wages had not been imposed on the retail trade industry, it is possible to estimate the number of retail trade workers who would have received less than the minimum wage that was in fact legislated. Using this estimate, it is easy to calculate the increase in the forecast wage that would result if all workers were paid at least the minimum wage. This measure and three alternatives are contained in table 11 and figure 1. The calculations in columns (1), (2), and (5) of table 11 all apply to employees of covered establishments. Column (1), for example, shows the proportionate increase in the mean forecast hourly rate of pay that would occur if all retail employees were paid at least the minimum rate of pay. If only covered establishments paid the minimum wage or more, then column (1) could be multiplied by the coverage rate (proportion of workers in covered establishments) to obtain a comparable figure for industry-wide average hourly earnings. Of course, insofar as the supply of workers to noncovered establishments is reduced by the prospect of receiving the minimum wage rate in covered employment, the appropriate calculation for the entire industry would approach that shown in column (1).

The measure contained in column (2), $\Delta' W_{rt}^*/W_{rt}^*$, is conceptually similar to that in column (1). It differs in the assumption that, instead of raising all subminimum wage workers to the minimum wage, the employer simply discharges them. As discussed above, this would result in a larger increase in the average wage bill than retaining all these workers while paying them the minimum. Column (3) is column (2) multiplied by the proportion of retail trade nonsupervisory employees in covered establishments. Column (4) simply shows the proportionate amount by which observed average hourly earnings in retail trade exceed the forecast figure. This quantity, which reflects the disemployment of subminimum employees and ripple effects, as well as errors in forecasting W_{rt}^*, is frequently much larger than $\Delta W_{rt}^*/W_{rt}^*$. Since $\Delta W_{rt}^*/W_{rt}^*$ is a good estimate of the impact of minimum wage legislation on average hourly earnings only if W_{rt}^* is a reasonably accurate forecast, it is comforting to note that column (2) is frequently larger, and never much smaller, than column (4). Column (3), reflecting partial coverage, always falls between column (1) and column (4). On the basis of these comparisons, it is not unwarranted to conclude that column (4) represents mainly the magnitude of direct minimum wage effects, layoffs, and ripple effects on the average wage in retail trade rather than forecasting error.

Contrast with Department of Labor Estimates. Column (5) contains the available estimates of the impact of minimum wage legislation on labor cost in retail trade prepared by the U.S. Department of Labor. These estimates are smaller than those of column (1).[10] The Department of Labor's estimates do not reflect either (1) the impact of anticipated federal minimum wage rates on labor cost or (2) the effect of existing minimum wage rates on the observed wage distribution.

To summarize, our best estimate of the proportionate increase in the mean wage necessary to pay all workers in covered retail trade establishments at least the minimum wage rate ranges from 2 percent in 1962, the first full year of coverage, up to a peak of 5.5 percent in 1968, falling to 2.1 percent in the last year for which data are available. Although this may not seem like a large quantity, it is much greater than estimates provided by the Department of Labor and roughly twice as large as my estimates for nonfarm industries outside retail trade (see table B1). In assessing the quantitative importance of these estimates, it is important to bear in mind that the base is the forecast mean wage for all retail trade nonsupervisory employees, whereas the affected workers are not average workers. A better picture of the size of the impact on the wage rates of directly affected workers is obtained by comparing the minimum wage with the mean forecast wage of workers earning less than the minimum W_{rm}^*.[11] The proportionate difference between the minimum wage—that is, the annual average minimum wage for all covered workers—and W_{rm}^* is 24.7 percent in 1962, 23.0 percent in 1968, and 24.3 percent in 1977. The increased price of low-productivity labor mandated by minimum wage legislation in retail trade is sizable indeed.

10 Column (1) is a yearly average. For the 1961 estimate in column (1) to be comparable with that in column (4), it should be multiplied by 3, since September-December is one-third of a year; the result is 0.021, which is over twice as large as the Department of Labor's figure for that year.

11 W_{rm}^* is calculated following a procedure similar to that used in obtaining the forecast wage.

TABLE 12

THE MEAN WAGE RATE IN COVERED RETAIL TRADE ESTABLISHMENTS RELATIVE TO NONCOVERED ESTABLISHMENTS, JUNE 1961 AND JUNE 1965

Year	*United States*	*Northeast*	*North Central*	*South*	*West*
1961	1.16	1.08	1.16	1.22	1.12
1965	1.14	1.04	1.15	1.21	1.12

SOURCE: U.S. Department of Labor, Wage and Hours and Public Contracts Divisions, *Retail Trade: A Study to Measure the Effects of the Minimum Wage and Maximum Hours Standards of the Fair Labor Standards Act* (1967).

Partial Coverage Once Again. As was pointed out above and in appendix A, a pronounced tendency for displaced workers to be absorbed in the noncovered sector would result in reduced or negligible disemployment for the industry, as well as a smaller or even zero increase in the industry average wage. Evidently, any tendency of disemployed workers to drive down wage rates in noncovered retail establishments is insufficiently important to offset completely increased wage rates in the covered sector. Table 12 supports this conclusion. For the United States as a whole, in June 1961 the mean wage rate in retail trade establishments that would become covered by federal minimum wage legislation in September 1961 was 16 percent greater than the mean rate in establishments that would remain noncovered. In June 1965, the average wage in covered establishments was only 14 percent greater than that in noncovered establishments.

Another comparison provides mixed evidence on whether employment shifts from the covered to the noncovered sector occurred, along with a resulting depression of the relative wage rate in noncovered employment. Gasoline service stations were essentially noncovered until rising gasoline prices in recent years pushed per station sales above the critical level (see table E1). The average wage rate for all retail trade relative to that in gasoline service stations was 1.17 in October 1956.[12] In June 1961, this ratio had risen to 1.25; by June 1965, it stood at 1.22.[13] It is possible that employers' anticipation of the minimum wage in 1961 forced workers into the noncovered sector, raising the ratio from 1.17 to 1.25. Why the wage ratio of all retail trade to gas stations would have fallen to 1.22 between 1961 and 1965 is unclear, however. It is also true that, within some divisions of

[12] U.S. Department of Labor, Bureau of Labor Statistics, *Employee Earnings in Retail Trade in October, 1956*, Bulletins 1220 and 1220-1 to 1220-7 (July 1957)

[13] U.S. Department of Labor, Wage and Hour and Public Contracts Divisions, *Retail Trade: An Interim Study of the Effects of the 1961 Amendments* (1966).

retail trade, the wage ratios of covered to noncovered establishments did increase after 1961. For variety stores, the ratio was 1.10 in 1961 and 1.30 in 1965. The ratio for drug stores rose from 1.08 to 1.13 and that for food stores from 1.35 to 1.40. A substantial part of these increases would have occurred simply because of minimum-wage-induced increases in the noncovered sectors of these divisions. Whatever employment displacement to noncovered retail trade did occur was evidently insufficient to offset substantially wage increases in the covered sector. Hence, we should expect federal minimum wage legislation to have caused a net reduction in employment for all retail trade compared with what would have been observed in the absence of wage regulation. We explore the extent of such disemployment in chapter 3.

Cost Offsets to Minimum Wage Rates and Noncompliance

The most careful measurement of the potential impact of minimum wage legislation on the cost of labor and the formulation of a model of its effect on employment would be largely beside the point if firms offset the minimum wage completely by reducing other labor costs or simply violated the law and did not pay workers the minimum. To some extent, cost offsets do occur. An examination of the relationship between wage supplements and federal minimum wage legislation applying to retail trade suggests a small but measurable reduction in these forms of wage payments when minimum wage rates increase. Details of this study are reported in appendix B. Chapter 4 presents evidence that in response to minimum wage legislation, firms reduce their allocation of resources to training inexperienced workers. There is no sure way of adding up all these offsets to minimum wages in order to balance them against the direct increase in wage costs. The negative employment impact reported in chapter 3 suggests, however, that whatever offsets do occur are by no means complete.

Compliance with federal minimum wage regulation cannot be determined with absolute accuracy, but available data suggest that it is sufficiently high so that the increased labor costs of compliance are an important economic variable.[14] The calculation of the impact of minimum wage regulation on the average cost of labor described in this chapter and in appendix B provides a convenient and appropriate means of estimating compliance with minimum wage regulation in

[14] For an analysis of compliance with minimum wage regulation in all industries taken together, see Orley Ashenfelter and Robert S. Smith, "Compliance with the Minimum Wage Law," *Journal of Political Economy*, vol. 87 (April 1979), pp. 333-50.

retail trade. An important part of this calculation involves estimating a statistical distribution function for wage rates in retail trade based on data from a survey made by the U.S. Department of Labor in 1956.[15] The second part of the calculation is based on a forecast mean wage for retail trade for the years 1961–1978. Combining the statistical distribution function with the forecast wage allows us to predict the proportion of workers that would have been paid less than any wage—the legal minimum, for example—had minimum wage legislation not altered the distribution of wages actually paid. The predicted proportion of workers receiving less than the minimum can be compared with information on the distribution of wages actually paid.

This comparison provides a measure of the degree of firms' compliance with federal minimum wage regulation. The information on wages actually paid was gathered from firms by the U.S. Department of Labor as part of a study of the impact of minimum wage legislation on the retail trade industry.[16] One problem with using this information for a study of compliance is that the firms surveyed may have feared prosecution if they reported paying their employees less than the minimum. Therefore, our measure of compliance may be too high. With this caveat in mind, we can measure compliance with minimum wage regulation in retail trade as follows. Let $A =$ the number of workers predicted to earn less than the minimum wage in retail trade, $B =$ the number actually earning less than the minimum, and $C =$ compliance. Then, a suitable measure of compliance is $C = (A - B)/A$. If compliance is perfect, then $B = 0$ and $C = 1$. If compliance is nonexistent, then $B = A$ and $C = 0$. Calculations of this measure of compliance for the United States and regions for all years in which data are available are shown in table 13. These calculations suggest a high measure of compliance with minimum wage regulation for all regions of the United States, with an increasing trend between 1962 and 1966. The amount of compliance suggested is higher than that reported by Orley Ashenfelter and Robert S. Smith.[17] One reason may be that their source of wage data is not from business firms, but from households. Although the firm data used in this study is potentially more accurate because firms are likely to keep better records of wage payments, there is the bias against reporting subminimum wage rates that could inflate the compliance measures

[15] U.S. Department of Labor, *Employee Earnings in Retail Trade in October, 1956.*

[16] U.S. Department of Labor, *Retail Trade: A Study of the Effects of the 1961 Amendments* (1967).

[17] Ashenfelter and Smith, "Compliance with the Minimum Wage Law."

reported in table 13. Even Ashenfelter and Smith report substantial compliance, however, and it seems highly unlikely that noncompliance with minimum wage regulation has been so great as to eliminate most costs of paying mandated higher rates of pay.

TABLE 13

COMPLIANCE WITH FEDERAL MINIMUM WAGE REGULATION IN RETAIL TRADE, 1962–1966

Year	*United States*	*Northeast*	*North Central*	*South*	*West*
1962	0.90	0.99	0.94	0.71	0.98
1965	0.94	0.99	0.96	0.78	1.0
1966	0.96	0.99	0.98	0.87	0.99

NOTE: For interpretation of the compliance measure, see text.
SOURCES: See text.

3

The Impact of Federal Minimum Wage Legislation on Employment and Hours of Work in Retail Trade

Explanations of why and how minimum wage rates affect employment have been woven into the general discussion of chapter 1 and the analysis of measuring the impact of a minimum wage on the cost of labor in chapter 2. Briefly, by raising the price an employer must pay for an input into the production process, a minimum wage rate reduces the quantity of that input demanded. Not only will there be substitution of other inputs in place of affected workers, but increased production costs will reduce the quantity of output and, consequently, the demand for all inputs. Although minimum wages affect mainly the demand for low-skilled and inexperienced workers, they may indirectly affect the quantity of higher-skilled workers demanded. Employers will have an incentive to increase the use of higher-quality, higher-priced labor in response to the legislated increase in the price of less-skilled workers. Working in the opposite direction, however, is the "scale" effect mentioned above; the increased costs induced by the minimum wage will lower the quantity of all inputs demanded. Thus, whether the quantity of higher-skilled workers demanded rises or falls depends on the outcome of these two opposing effects of a minimum wage rate.

Available data do not permit a detailed analysis of the way in which employment of workers by skill or experience level is affected by minimum wage rates in individual industries. Therefore, the bulk of this chapter is devoted to an analysis of what has happened to the quantity of all labor employed in retail trade as a result of minimum wage legislation. To supplement this study of the aggregate demand for retail trade labor, we do explore the impact on a group of low-wage workers who are likely to be particularly affected by minimum wage regulation: young persons aged fourteen- to twenty-four years. Much of what we know about the retail trade industry and youth employment patterns suggests that this group of workers has suffered a particularly severe reduction in their opportunities for employment as a result of extension of minimum wage coverage to retail trade.[1]

The Demand for Labor in Retail Trade and Minimum Wages

More than one approach can be followed in estimating the impact of minimum wage rates on the quantity of labor demanded in an industry or group of industries. Three approaches are followed in this study. The technical details of these research strategies are discussed at length in appendix C, along with all of the statistical results. Here we summarize the estimates of the effect of minimum wage rates on the quantity of labor demanded in retail trade and outline the methods by which they are obtained.

Correlation. The simplest method, and the one that perhaps seems most obvious, is simply to observe whether retail trade employment falls when retail trade minimum wage rates go up. Of course, it is necessary to control for whether wage rates paid to retail employees would have risen in any event and for other important conditions impinging on retail employment that were changing at the same time as minimum wage rates. We call this direct method the correlation approach. As used in this study, the correlation approach involves relating the amount of retail trade employment divided by the U.S. population to three variables: (1) a variable measuring the impact of the retail trade minimum wage on the cost of retail trade labor; (2) a variable measuring general business conditions; and (3) a trend variable designed to capture the effects of other, unmeasured conditions influencing the demand for labor in retail trade.

The numerator of the dependent variable takes two forms: (1) the number of retail trade employees, and (2) the product of the number of employees and average weekly hours of work, called "total hours." Interestingly, the implications of the minimum wage for a reduction in employment holds strictly only for the second measure, total hours. In response to an increase in hourly wage costs, employers may find that it is economical to increase the number of part-time workers while reducing full-time employment, so that total hours fall while the number of workers employed may actually increase.[2]

[1] See Finis Welch, "Minimum Wage Legislation in the United States," in Orley Ashenfelter and James Blum, eds., *Evaluating the Labor Market Effects of Social Programs* (Princeton, N.J.: Princeton University Industrial Relations Section, 1977), pp. 14-23; and the discussion in chapter 2.

[2] M. Ishaq Nadiri and Sherwin Rosen, *A Disequilibrium Model of Demand for Factors of Production*, National Bureau of Economic Research General Series no. 99 (New York: National Bureau of Economic Research, 1973), chapter 2.

The minimum wage variable is also represented by two versions: (a) the ratio of the minimum wage to the average wage in retail trade multiplied by the proportion of workers in covered establishments, and (b) the proportional increase in the forecast retail trade average wage that would be required to pay all subminimum wage workers the minimum wage. Version (b) is $\Delta W_{rt}^*/W_{rt}^*$, described in chapter 2 and shown in table 11, column (1). The variable representing general business conditions is the unemployment rate of males aged thirty-five to fifty-four. This measure of unemployment is a good representative of the overall state of the economy and is unlikely to be affected by minimum wage rates. The third variable is one commonly used in studies of events that occur over time. It takes on the value of 1 in the earliest time period (year) used in the analysis and increases by 1 for each subsequent year.

The Demand for Labor. The second and third approaches to estimating the impact of minimum wage rates on employment use the formal framework of what economists call a factor, or input, demand model. This study uses two variants of a factor demand equation. Although it is not as obvious or simple a procedure as the correlation approach, the factor demand approach has the merit, at least in theory, of considering all the conditions that systematically influence the demand for labor. If this presumption is correct, then this approach may measure the impact of a minimum wage on employment more reliably than the correlation approach.

The demand for labor in the retail trade industry is formulated from the point of view of the consumer. The consumer, or household, demands goods and the services provided by the retail trade industry to achieve its consumption goals. Since the services provided by retail establishments are produced with labor and nonlabor inputs, it is consumers who ultimately decide how many of these inputs retail firms will purchase or employ. In a fundamental sense, retail firms are simply intermediaries carrying out consumer desires.

In the first variant of the factor demand equation, consumers are viewed as basing their decisions about how much retail labor to hire on four variables: (1) their spendable incomes in terms of constant dollars, (2) the price of retail labor, (3) the cost of goods to retailers, and (4) the price of all other inputs into the retail and household production processes as represented by a catch-all trend variable. The rationale underlying this formulation is that the demand for any productive input depends on the level of production, the price of the input, and the prices of all other inputs used with it. The level of production in this case is the volume of (unobservable) consumption, which is determined by consumers' purchasing power and by costs.

The cost of consumption is determined by factor prices, given technology. The factors of production other than labor include goods, other inputs used by retail firms, and the consumer's own time.

Ideally, the price of all these factors other than labor would be included explicitly in the factor demand equation. Unfortunately, data limitations and the statistical problem that the prices of the factors move closely together over time make the ideal impractical. That is why the trend variable is used to capture the effects on consumer decisions of factor prices other than the prices of retail labor and goods.

The variable of greatest interest in all this is, of course, the price of retail labor. This is measured by the forecast average wage rate in retail trade plus the amount required to pay all workers at least the minimum wage. In terms of the variables developed in chapter 2, the price of labor is measured by $W_{rt}^* + \Delta W_{rt}^*$. Measurement of the price of goods is defined in appendix C.

A second variant of the factor demand equation is adopted because of conceptual and statistical problems involved with the first version. In both the first and second versions of the equation, minimum wage effects are inferred from the estimated relationship between a variable representing the price of retail labor and the quantity of retail labor. For this approach to be valid, an increase in the price of labor resulting from the minimum wage must affect the quantity of labor demanded in a manner identical to an equal increase in the mean wage resulting from any other cause. As noted above, the construction of the retail wage variable depends in large part on the average wage paid workers in durable goods manufacturing. It is thus highly correlated with the wage paid to the average worker in the labor force. This means that, even though purchasing power as represented by real disposable income is included as a variable in the factor demand equation, it is not unlikely that an increase in the wage variable reflects increased purchasing power in its own right, as well as an increase in the price of retail labor. Thus, an increase in the wage variable may be positively associated with the quantity of retail labor because of the variable's possible correlation with purchasing power, as well as negatively associated with the quantity of labor because it is a measure of labor's cost.

While an increase in the minimum wage also raises the spendable income of workers who retain their jobs, these workers represent a very small proportion of total spending power because (1) the minimum wage directly affects only a fraction of the labor force overall, and (2) many directly affected workers lose their jobs and thus do not experience increased earnings as a result of the minimum wage.

Therefore, an increase in the minimum wage has mainly a price effect on the quantity of labor demanded and a negligible income effect.

The second variant of the factor demand equation avoids the positive feedback of wage rates to the quantity of labor demanded through retail sales via the income effect by using the ratio of labor employed to retail sales as the dependent variable rather than simply the quantity of labor demanded. The wage variable is modified to reflect the ratio of the wage variable used in the first variant to the variable reflecting the price of goods paid by retailers.

A Mixed Approach. A difficulty with both variants of the factor demand equation is that each relates the aggregate quantity of labor employed in retail trade to one variable representing labor's price, whereas most retail firms employ workers of various skill and experience levels, each affected differently by minimum wages. Although available data do not permit modification of the labor demand equations to examine the impact of minimum wage rates on different classes of workers, a mixed procedure including both the minimum wage variable $\Delta W_{rt}^*/W_{rt}^*$ used in the correlation approach and the forecast retail wage as separate variables permits separate but simultaneous analyses of the impact of an increase in the average cost of retail labor and an increase in the cost of low-wage labor due to the minimum wage. Because it provides a test of the robustness of the results obtained using the correlation and factor demand approaches, statistical analysis has also been carried out with the mixed approach.

The Impact of Minimum Wage Rates on Employment in Retail Trade

A detailed statistical analysis of the three approaches to estimating the impact of federal minimum wage regulation on employment in retail trade is contained in appendix C. The major thrust of the results of this empirical investigation is presented here.

One of the most important results is that all three approaches imply a significant reduction in retail trade employment attributable to minimum wage legislation. The first variant of the factor demand equation approach suggests a smaller impact than do the other procedures. Since we have reasons for believing that conceptual and statistical problems associated with the first variant are likely to lead to an underestimate (in absolute terms) of the relationship between wage rates and employment, the results summarized here are based on the correlation approach and the second variant of the factor demand approach (which focuses on the ratio of retail labor to retail sales). Results of the mixed approach generally corroborate those obtained using the correlation and factor demand (second variant) procedures.

The various approaches to estimating the employment effects of minimum wage legislation were carried out, not only for all retail trade (except eating and drinking places) taken together, but also for several important subindustries of retail trade, including department stores, variety stores, food stores, drug stores, and apparel stores. (Not all of these results are published here.) The branches of retail trade within which minimum wage regulation appears to have had a particularly strong impact on employment are variety stores and food stores. While I suspect that employment in gasoline stations also has been substantially affected in recent years, data are unavailable to study this industry in the same way as other parts of retail trade. Although we have not developed a model of the retail trade industry that is sufficiently rich in institutional detail to permit a thorough understanding of why some divisions of retail trade are more severely affected by minimum wage legislation than others, casual observation of the importance of labor costs and the highly competitive nature of food and variety stores lead one to choose these as particularly likely to economize on labor in response to increased wage rates.

The statistical results presented in appendix C suggest that the impact of minimum wages on department store employment has, at first sight, been negligible. Closer examination, however, suggests that minimum wage legislation has actually resulted in an expansion of employment in department stores relative to the rest of retail trade and, within the general merchandise group, relative to variety stores. It is suggested in appendix C that the reason for this expansionary impact is that department stores are more able than others to economize on labor costs by centralizing locations at which patrons pay for their purchases, mechanizing and computerizing shelf stocking and inventory controls, and so on; thus, while they have probably cut back on the amount of labor employed per dollar of sales, they have experienced sufficient sales growth relative to all retail trade that their share of total employment has grown as well.

Disemployment Resulting from Minimum Wage Regulation. In this section, some of the results of the statistical analysis described in appendix C are used to estimate the actual reduction in the quantity of labor hired by retail firms that has resulted from the minimum wage regulation. These estimates are presented in table 14 for all retail trade and for food stores, which accounted for about 22 percent of all nonsupervisory employees in retail trade except eating and drinking places in 1978. Disemployment estimates are not shown for the other large branch of retail trade analyzed in appendix C (department and variety stores). This is because the statistical evidence on the relationship between the wage variable and employment as measured by total hours per capita is very sensitive to whether the trend variable is included in the input demand equation (second variant). This may be because of changes over time in the way sales have been allocated among the various subcategories of retail trade, but we have no way of ascertaining whether this is so.

Table 14 is read in this way: The source column shows the statistical estimate in appendix C from which the calculation in each row is derived. Column (1) contains the estimated percentage impact on employment of a minimum wage rate that raises the average wage paid to all workers by 1 percent. For example, the number 0.87 in the first row of column (1) in section A indicates that a minimum wage that would raise the average hourly rate of pay (if all workers below the minimum were raised to the minimum) from, say, $4.00 to $4.04, would result in 0.87 percent fewer retail trade employees than there would have been in the absence of a minimum wage. In order to translate this estimate into an actual change in employment, it is necessary to multiply the number in column (1) by the numbers in columns (2) and (3). Finally, in column (4) we show the disemployment resulting from a minimum wage that increases the average hourly rate of pay by 5 percent from, say, $4.00 to $4.20 (this is about the value of $\Delta W_{rt}^*/W_{rt}^*$ that prevailed during the 1968–1970 period). The result is almost 325,000 workers, or about 4.5 percent of the number of nonsupervisory retail trade employees.

Section B of table 14 is read in the same way as section A, except that the measure of the quantity of labor is the number of workers multiplied by average weekly hours of work. To facilitate comparison of the numbers in section B, column (4), with those in section A, the former are divided by 35 (average weekly hours of work). In the opening section of this chapter, it was pointed out that total hours of employment should be reduced more in response to an increase in the minimum wage than in the number of employees. This seems to be the case, for a comparison of row 5 with row 1 shows over a 70 percent greater reduction in total hours hired by retail trade firms than in the number of workers employed.

Rows 2 and 6 of table 14 show the estimated effect of an increase in the minimum wage on employment based on the second variant of the input demand approach. Since the measure of the quantity of labor in this approach is the ratio of employment (or total hours) to retail sales, these estimates do not allow for any effect of increased

TABLE 14

DISEMPLOYMENT RESULTING FROM A MINIMUM WAGE THAT RAISES THE FORECAST MEAN WAGE RATE BY 5 PERCENT

Row	Source (table/row)	*Change in per Capita Employment or in Employment-Sales Ratio Due to a 1 Percent Increase in the Forecast Mean Wage Rate (percent)* (1)	*Mean per Capita Employment (1960–1978)* (2)	*Mean Population (1960–1978)* (3)	$(1)\times(2)\times(3)\times 0.05$	
					Change in employment (4)	Sales held constant?
			Retail Trade			
1	C1/2	−0.87	0.037	201,700,000	−324,636	No
2	C2/4	−0.60	0.037	201,700,000	−223,887	Yes
			Food Stores			
3	C6/1	−0.62	0.0078	201,700,000	− 97,542	No
4	C6/5	−0.69	0.0078	201,700,000	−108,554	Yes

		Change in per Capita Total Hours or in Total Hours-Sales Ratio Due to a 1 Percent Increase in the Forecast Mean Wage Rate (percent) *(1)*	*Mean per Capita Total Hours (1960–1968)* *(2)*	*Mean Population (1960–1978)* *(3)*	$\frac{(1) \times (2) \times (3) \times 0.05}{35}$ Change in total hours in worker equivalents (4)	Sales held constant?
			Retail Trade			
5	C1/4	−1.50	1.32	201,700,000	−570,523	No
6	C2/5	−0.70	1.32	201,700,000	−266,244	Yes
			Food Stores			
7	C6/2	−0.81	0.26	201,700,000	− 60,682	No
8	C6/9	−0.65	0.26	201,700,000	− 48,696	Yes

SOURCES: Tables C1, C2, and C6.

labor costs on consumers' retail purchases. When the cost of retail services rises, consumers are likely to curtail their purchases of goods through retail outlets. Some clothes that had been bought in apparel or department stores, for example, may be sewn at home. Food items may be grown by the consumers instead of purchased in stores. Car owners may do more of their own servicing and minor repairs. Thus, when sales are held constant as they are in this approach, the estimated impact of a minimum wage increase on the quantity of labor demanded should be less than when sales are not held constant. The estimates shown in rows 2 and 6 are considerably smaller than their counterparts in rows 1 and 5, suggesting a substantial negative impact of increased labor costs on retail sales as well as on the number of employees hired to service a given volume of retail transactions.

The evidence on food stores suggests that a 5 percent increase in the forecast wage attributable to an increase in the minimum wage reduced the quantity of labor hired by around 100,000 workers when the number of workers employed is the measure of the demand for labor. This is about 7 percent of the labor force of nonsupervisory personnel employed in food stores over the period studied. Contrary to expectations and to the results for all retail trade, when total hours is the measure of labor demanded, the reduction in employment is roughly half as large as when the number of workers is the measure of the quantity of labor. Moreover, the evidence on whether food store sales, as well as employment per dollar of sales, are reduced by minimum wage legislation is conflicting. A comparison of rows 7 and 8 of table 14 suggests that sales are curtailed, whereas a comparison of rows 3 and 4 implies that they are not.

The results of the detailed empirical study reported in appendix C and summarized here are that there is little doubt that minimum wage regulation has curtailed employment in retail trade. Although the precise magnitude of such a relationship is always more uncertain than its direction, a reasonable interpretation of the study is that on the average during the 1960's, when minimum wages boosted the average cost of labor by about 5 percent, the amount of labor hired was over 5 percent less than it would have been in the absence of a federal minimum wage law.

The Effect of Minimum Wages on Employment and Unemployment of Young Persons

We present here a brief summary of the effects of minimum wage rates in retail trade on the employment and unemployment experience of young persons aged fourteen to twenty-four. The procedure parallels what we have called the correlation approach to estimating the effect of minimum wage rates on the demand for retail labor; a more detailed discussion is contained in appendix C.

Briefly, the study of employment and unemployment is carried out as follows. The employment rate or unemployment rate (per capita employment or unemployment) is statistically related to the retail trade minimum wage variable used in the correlation approach to estimating the impact of retail trade minimum wage rates on the demand for retail labor, $\Delta W_{rt}^*/W_{rt}^*$. In addition, other variables likely to influence the job opportunities and hence the employment or unemployment of young persons are included in the analysis. These variables include a measure of the impact of minimum wage rates on the cost of labor in industries other than retail trade, the proportion of persons aged fifteen to twenty-four in the U.S. population, the size of the armed forces relative to the population, the unemployment rate of adult men (a measure of general business conditions), and a trend variable used to capture the effects of unknown forces influencing job opportunities and employment behavior. We are thus estimating the relationship between employment, or unemployment, and minimum wage rates in retail trade, net of all the influences represented in these additional variables.

These employment and unemployment relationships were estimated over two time periods, 1948–1978 and 1960–1978, with the latter period focusing more closely on the years since federal minimum wage legislation has been effective in retail trade. Table 15 summarizes the results for those age groups that, on the basis of both the 1947–1978 and the 1960–1978 estimates, experienced a significant impact of minimum wage rates in *retail trade* on their employment or unemployment. If the estimated relationship implies that minimum wage rates in retail trade affect employment or unemployment, but that the effect of minimum wage rates in other industries is opposite in sign, statistically significant, and substantially offsetting in magnitude, then the results are not summarized in table 15.

Males eighteen and nineteen years old and females fourteen to seventeen years old appear to have experienced significant disemployment associated with minimum wage rates in retail trade. The total disemployment for these two age groups, based on 1970 population figures, has been over 420,000 individuals. This is a larger number than the total reduction in the number of retail trade employees reported in table 14, but it is by no means inconsistent with those figures. It simply suggests that some young employees have been replaced with older workers. The disemployment for males aged eighteen and nineteen represents about 9 percent of their average

TABLE 15

YOUNG PERSONS' DISEMPLOYMENT AND UNEMPLOYMENT ASSOCIATED WITH A MINIMUM WAGE THAT RAISES THE FORECAST MEAN WAGE RATE BY 5 PERCENT

Group	*Row*	*Source (row in table C7)*	*Change in per Capita Employment[a] (percent) (1)*	*1970 Population (2)*	*(1)×(2)×0.05 Change in Employment or Unemployment (3)*
			Disemployment		
Males, 18–19 years old	1	6	−1.12	3,655,678	−204,718
Females, 14–17 years old	2	12	−0.56	7,776,315	−217,736
			Unemployment		
Males, 14–17 years old	3	20	−0.43	8,063,073	−173,356
Males, 18–19 years old	4	22	−0.58	3,655,678	−106,014

[a] The data describe the change associated with a 1 percent increase in the forecast mean wage rate.

SOURCES: Table C7 and U.S. Bureau of the Census, *Census of Population: 1970*, vol. 1, *Characteristics of the Population*, part 1, *U.S. Summary*, section 1, table 50.

employment rate over the 1960–1978 period, and for females aged fourteen to seventeen about 14 percent.

Unemployment for young males, both those fourteen to seventeen and those eighteen and nineteen, appears to have been reduced by minimum wage rates in retail trade. Although it may be customary to think of minimum wage rates as increasing unemployment, only the reduction in employment is predicted unambiguously by economic analysis.[3] Unemployment may rise or fall, depending on how severely the disemployed are discouraged from looking for jobs in the noncovered sector or waiting for covered jobs to open up. Thus, the esti-

[3] Jacob Mincer, "Unemployment Effects of Minimum Wages," *Journal of Political Economy*, vol. 84, no. 4, part 2 (August 1976), pp. S87-S104.

mates summarized in table 15 show that, overall, minimum wages in retail trade have curtailed the labor force participation (employment and unemployment taken together) of teenagers of both sexes. This represents not only lost current output to society but also a potentially serious future loss arising from the diminished labor force experience of these young people. A further examination of the impact of minimum wages on the future earning power of young men is contained in chapter 4.

4

Long-Run Effects on the Acquisition of Schooling, Training, and Wage Growth

So far, we have considered only the direct effect of minimum wage legislation on the cost of labor, employment, and unemployment. In addition to these short-run effects, minimum wage regulation is likely to affect employer and worker activities that influence the type and amount of activity aimed at development of labor market skills and, hence, future wage rates. In this chapter, we briefly consider such long-run effects of minimum wage rates in the retail trade industry.

Schooling, Training, and Human Capital

Little justification is needed to assert that among the most important economic activities are the various formal and informal training activities that develop worker productivity and provide the foundation for the lion's share of wage growth over an individual worker's lifetime. Schooling is a type of formal training that aims, as one of its most important functions, to increase worker productivity through the acquisition of verbal and quantitative skills. These qualities enhance a worker's value to employers directly, and indirectly they provide a basis upon which on-the-job training can further increase productivity. Both schooling and training are properly considered to be investments by workers in themselves and by firms who expect to benefit from the enhanced skills of their employees. Thus, they are often referred to by economists as activities that increase human capital.[1]

[1] For a presentation of the theory of human capital and references to the scientific literature in this area, see Belton M. Fleisher and Thomas J. Kniesner, *Labor Economics: Theory, Evidence, and Policy*, 2nd ed. (Englewood Cliffs, N.J.: Prentice-Hall, 1980), chapters 8 and 9.

Training that occurs in the course of working at a job is less easily observed and measured than schooling, but it is probably equally important in determining a worker's earning power. It is helpful to think of a typical firm not only as hiring workers to produce output in exchange for wages, but also as selling training to its employees in return for their services. This is particularly true in the case of young workers, whose early labor market experiences will shape their work habits and abilities throughout the remainder of their working lives. Since retail trade is such an important employer of young persons, it is an important provider of on-the-job training for workers who eventually find employment in all industries. Consequently, any form of regulation that impinges on the retail labor force is likely to have important long-run implications for the entire economy.

How Investment in Human Capital Occurs. Schooling and on-the-job training are viewed as investments because they involve paying a cost in exchange for expected returns in the future. In the case of school, the major costs include direct expenditures on tuition and the implicit cost of forgone earnings in the labor market. For grammar school and high school students attending public institutions, and for those enrolled in publicly supported colleges and universities, forgone earnings account for the bulk of investment costs. Even students attending private colleges and universities where tuition now approaches $10,000 a year probably could earn that much if they were full-time workers and not students. Thus, even for them, indirect costs probably account for about one-half of total expenditures on acquiring a college degree. Although many high school and college students hold jobs while they are enrolled and full-time jobs during the summer, their rate of pay is typically lower than if they were employed full-time all year long.

Young persons and their families are willing to bear these investment costs if they expect the future returns to be sufficient to warrant the current sacrifice. Thus, an increase in the earning power of high school graduates relative to that of college graduates would induce some potential college students to enter the full-time labor force immediately after leaving high school rather than pursue a college degree. Similarly, an increase in the salaries of college graduates, other things equal, would lead to increased college attendance.

Investment decisions in on-the-job training follow the same principles as investment in schooling, but the measures for costs and returns are perhaps somewhat less obvious. These measurements are based on the plausible assumption that all jobs offer pay in at least two forms: (1) a money wage and (2) the opportunity to develop skills and knowledge that will enable the worker to earn a higher wage in the future. This second component of the pay package is valuable to a job-holder and is particularly important to young workers who learn not only occupation-specific skills, but also general knowledge of the world of work, including punctuality, employer-employee relationships, how to get along with fellow workers, pride in workmanship, and so on.

Because training is valuable, many workers will accept a job at a relatively low initial rate of pay if it offers sufficient opportunity to earn higher wages later on. Indeed, competition for such jobs will force initial rates of pay down below the wages that can be earned in jobs that offer less, or no, expectation of future wage growth. Thus, the cost of training to a worker is the amount by which initial wages fall short of opportunities that offer less training; the returns are determined by greater earning power later on. There is a close correspondence between the opportunity cost of on-the-job training and the indirect component (forgone earnings) of schooling costs. Similarly, the returns to both forms of investment in human capital consist of increased earning power after the investments have been made.

Minimum Wage Rates and Investment in Human Capital. By raising wage rates employers must pay to many employees, particularly young workers, minimum wage legislation is likely to affect the most important stage of investing in human capital. Both schooling and on-the-job training decisions are likely to be affected by legal wage floors.

Schooling and minimum wages. Minimum wage rates can either increase or decrease the amount of schooling chosen by an individual. A penetrating analysis by Ronald Ehrenberg and Alan Marcus shows that, because part-time, student employees generally receive lower rates of pay than they would as full-time, year-round workers, minimum wage legislation is likely to increase the difficulty many individuals and their families face in financing further education.[2] Thus, the children of low-income families especially may be induced to forgo schooling and enter the labor market full time because minimum wage legislation increases the difficulty of finding a job while enrolled in school. On the other hand, many full-time workers earn less than

[2] Ronald G. Ehrenberg and Alan Marcus, "Minimum Wage Legislation and the Educational Decisions of Youths: Perpetuation of Income Inequality across Generations?" in Simon Rottenberg, ed., *The Economics of Legal Minimum Wages* (Washington, D.C.: American Enterprise Institute, forthcoming).

the minimum wage. The reduced employment opportunities for these persons may induce them to acquire more schooling because (1) they may view the increased difficulty in finding work (even though at a higher wage) sufficiently burdensome that the opportunity cost of schooling is reduced, and (2) schooling will raise the wage they expect to earn later on and thus reduce the impact of the minimum wage on their future employment opportunities.

To summarize, minimum wage regulation may increase or decrease school attendance. The impact on schooling, however, is unlikely to be neutral across families in different income classes. Those who need part-time work opportunities to support themselves while attending school because they have little wealth are most likely to leave school to enter the labor force, thus reducing the likelihood that their relative economic position will improve.

Ehrenberg and Marcus investigate the extent to which this perverse impact of minimum wage legislation occurs by using data on schooling decisions of young persons who live in different states of the United States and who are thus affected differently by minimum wage legislation because of variation in normal wage levels and state minimum wage laws.[3] Their study yields conflicting results on this important issue. In another study, J. Peter Mattila finds that, on balance, increases in the minimum wage over time increase school attendance by teenagers.[4]

On-the-job training and minimum wages. The human capital frame of analysis implies that, if employers are forced to increase the amount they pay workers who had been benefiting from on-the-job training, they will endeavor to reduce their labor costs by cutting back on the degree to which their jobs offer training opportunities. In the absence of minimum wage legislation, for example, new workers may receive extra supervision from senior workers, which reduces the output of the latter. This reduced output is a cost of training and may be paid for by the new workers in the form of reduced wages. Competition among firms will assure that the amount by which wages are reduced does not exceed the firms' training costs. If firms reduce the amount of resources devoted to training their new workers, then the observed rate of pay may be raised when they are paid the minimum wage, but in the long run they may be no better off—or even worse off—because they do not receive training that would have increased their pay over time.

---

[3] Ibid.

[4] J. Peter Mattila, "The Impact of Minimum Wages on Teenage Schooling and on the Part-Time/Full-Time Employment of Youths," in Rottenberg, ed., *The Economics of Legal Minimum Wages.*

What if on-the-job training does not actually cost the firm anything, in that no resources are specifically reallocated toward supervision of new workers or formal training programs? Rather, new workers are simply less efficient than experienced workers, and on-the-job training occurs through learning by doing? A new worker, for example, may produce a smaller output per day than an experienced worker, or cause more waste, or the new worker's output may have to be redone more frequently than that of an experienced worker. Lower wage rates of young workers reflect lower efficiency, and actual work experience (as opposed to simply growing older) is required to increase productivity. If jobs differ in the extent to which they offer the opportunity to improve, individuals seeking work must choose between those jobs that offer training opportunities and those that do not. Employers will not pay employees more than they are "worth," but workers will accept low wages in jobs providing learning by doing because of the prospective wage increases that would not occur in alternative employment. These alternative jobs will, in general, pay more to beginning workers than those in which learning takes place, but they do not reflect better long-run opportunities because little expected wage growth is associated with them.

Imposing a wage floor above the amount paid to beginning workers means that employers will hire fewer of them. Opportunities to obtain jobs in which learning by doing occurs will be reduced, although those lucky individuals who obtain these jobs will be better off than before. Others will be forced to take jobs that do not offer learning opportunities. Such jobs may not be directly affected by minimum wage legislation because they offer higher rates of pay to new workers as compensation for negligible impact on future earning power.

Full Wage Rates Versus Observed Wage Rates. The concept of investment in human capital leads us to focus broadly on the pattern of wage payments over an individual's working life rather than narrowly, at a moment in time. When we do this, it becomes apparent that the observed rate of pay is distinct from what might be called the full wage. The latter reflects not only current payments in cash and fringe benefits, but also the effect of current work experience on future increases in earning power. Although it may seem difficult to measure an individual's full wage, data exist that permit us to measure it to a fairly close approximation.[5]

[5] The method used here was developed by Edward Lazear. See, for example, his "Age, Experience, and Wage Growth," *American Economic Review*, vol. 66, no. 4, (September 1976), pp. 548-58; and his "The Narrowing of Black-White Wage Differentials Is Illusory," *American Economic Review*, vol. 69, no. 4 (September 1969), pp. 553-64.

"Longitudinal" labor market surveys are available for various age-sex groups within the U.S. population. A longitudinal survey provides information on wage rates and work experience for a given group of individuals over a period of years. Thus, it is possible to relate work experience in one year to wage growth over several subsequent years.

Calculating the full wage rate. The following example shows how an individual's full wage can be measured using data from a longitudinal survey. Suppose we have information on two individuals who are identical in every respect except their work experience. Both individuals work during year one and would earn $\$X$ per hour at the beginning of year two if they chose to work. One of the individuals (A) works during year two and the other (B) does not, but resumes work in year three. By comparing the wage rates of the two individuals at the beginning of year three, we can infer the impact of a year of work experience on earning power.[6] Suppose that, at the beginning of year three, individual A earns $\$X\ (1 + n)$ per hour, while individual B earns $\$X\ (1 + m)$ per hour, where m is less than n. The difference $\$X(n - m)$ is the effect of a year of experience on hourly earnings.

To calculate an approximate measure of the full wage rate during year two, we assume that the training individual A received during year two will allow him to earn $\$X(n - m)$ more than he would otherwise have earned throughout his working life. Suppose that A is twenty-five years old, that he can be expected to work another forty years after year two at a rate of 2,000 hours a year, and that he worked 2,000 hours during year two. Thus, each hour that A worked in year two added $[\$X(n - m) \div 2{,}000] \times 2{,}000 \times 40 = \$X(n - m) \times 40$ to his lifetime earnings. $\$X(n - m) \times 40$ is like an annuity received by A for each hour of work in year two. Thus, we calculate the amount it would cost to purchase such an annuity—the present value of the income stream $\$X(n - m) \times 40$—and add it to $\$X$. $\$X$ plus the present value of $\$X(n - m) \times 40$ is an approximate measure of individual A's full wage in year two.

The effect of a minimum wage. Suppose now that another identical individual, C, worked during years one and two, but that during year two he worked at a job covered by minimum wage legislation and earned $\$Y$ per hour, where $\$Y$ is the minimum wage and exceeds $\$X$. By observing what C earns at the beginning of year three, we

[6] This is an approximation, because we never observe directly how much the full wage grows, but only how much the observed wage grows. Nevertheless, the difference in the rate of growth of observed and full wage rates is probably not large enough to create serious difficulties with this approach. See Lazear, "The Narrowing of Black-White Wage Differentials," pp. 554–57.

can calculate his full wage during year two by following the procedure outlined in the preceding paragraphs. A comparison of *C*'s full wage with that of *A* will provide a more accurate measure of the effect of minimum wage legislation on *C*'s economic well-being than a comparison of their observed wage rates during year two. It is apparent that, although *Y* exceeds *X*, *C*'s full wage need not exceed *A*'s, because *Y*'s wage growth may fall short of *X*'s wage growth.

The Effect of Minimum Wage Rates in Retail Trade on Investment in Human Capital

In the remainder of this chapter, we explore the impact of minimum wage rates in retail trade on investment in human capital. We first investigate whether minimum wage rates in retail trade have, on balance, tended to increase or reduce school attendance. As mentioned previously, Peter Mattila has found that minimum wage legislation in all industries taken together has resulted in increased school attendance.[7] Our focus here is on the particular role of federal minimum wage regulation in retail trade on schooling decisions of young persons. Second, we explore the impact of minimum wage regulation on the relationship between work experience and wage growth. This relationship has also been studied by Jacob Mincer and Linda Leighton.[8] They use variation in minimum wage coverage by state and variation in the ratio of the minimum wage to the average state wage as a measure of the impact of minimum wage regulation, and they find a negative impact of minimum wage rates on wage growth. Their data, which come from two separate longitudinal surveys, permit them to analyze wage growth over three separate time periods. (Their use of state wage data is similar to that of Ehrenberg and Marcus.) Our study uses a minimum wage measure that is industry-specific; thus, the impact of minimum wage regulation in the retail trade industry on wage growth can be implicitly measured.

Ideally, we would like to estimate the combined impact of minimum wage rates on investment in human capital via schooling and training. Minimum wages may reduce human capital accumulation obtained via training but increase accumulation via schooling. Unfortunately, it would be extremely difficult to measure the impact of minimum wages on the ultimate amount of schooling obtained by an individual, as opposed to estimating the impact simply on school

7 Mattila, "The Impact of Minimum Wages on Teenage Schooling."

8 Jacob Mincer and Linda Leighton, "Effect of Minimum Wages on Human Capital Formation," Working Paper no. 441 (Cambridge, Mass.: National Bureau of Economic Research, February 1980).

attendance, and measurement of this minimum wage impact has not been attempted.

Even if we knew how much additional schooling is obtained by individuals whose labor market opportunities are reduced by legal wage floors, it would not be a straightforward task to infer the quantitative, or even the qualitative, impact on human capital accumulation. Some individuals who attend school in response to the impact of minimum wage legislation on their job opportunities substitute full-time schooling for full-time work and drop out of the labor force entirely, while others obtain part-time jobs while they attend school.[9] Both of these groups are substituting one form of investment in human capital (formal schooling) for another (on-the-job training), the former group to a greater extent than the latter. But what is the value of human capital obtained via schooling for these individuals? To answer this question accurately would require lifetime data on their wage rates after leaving school, and it would be misleading to assume that they benefit from schooling to the same extent as those who choose school over market work independently of the influence of minimum wages. Presumably, one reason for an individual's ending his schooling and entering the labor market while others go on to acquire further formal education is a judgment that more can be gained from on-the-job training than from schooling. Those who choose the schooling route to further investment in human capital, on the other hand, presumably believe that is the most rewarding route for them. That is, individuals differ in their capacities to benefit from schooling and on-the-job training. Those who shift from one path to the other are thus pursuing what for them is a second-best course. They will more likely benefit less from the form of investment in human capital chosen in response to the impact of minimum wage legislation than those who would have chosen that form in any event. This "comparative advantage" view of variation in the benefits from schooling among individuals is analyzed in depth and supported empirically in recent research.[10]

Because of the conceptual and factual difficulties enumerated above, no attempt has been made to assess the total impact of minimum wage regulation in retail trade on investment in human capital. First, we estimate the impact on schooling. Second, we report estimates of the impact on the relationship between work experience and wage growth, both for work experience obtained while attending school and for experience while not pursuing formal education. Esti-

[9] See Mattila, "The Impact of Minimum Wages on Teenage Schooling."

[10] Robert J. Willis and Sherwin Rosen, "Education and Self Selection," *Journal of Political Economy*, vol. 87, no. 5, part 2 (October 1979), pp. S7-S36.

mates of the full wage as influenced by minimum wage rates are also presented.

Minimum Wages in Retail Trade and Investment in Human Capital

In the remainder of this chapter, estimates of the impact of minimum wages in retail trade on investment in human capital are presented. We begin with the association between minimum wage rates and schooling decisions and then discuss the impact of minimum wage legislation on on-the-job training and full wage rates.

Minimum Wage Rates and Schooling. Using a related but distinct approach from that used here, Mattila has shown that, when the federal minimum wage rate has been increased and/or coverage expanded, school attendance among teenagers is increased moderately.[11] Can an independent effect of minimum wage regulation in retail trade be distinguished? This question is addressed in detail in appendix D, and a brief summary of findings is presented here. There does appear to be a significant impact of minimum wages in retail trade on the schooling decisions of eighteen- and nineteen-year-olds of both sexes. This is after the impact of federal minimum wage regulation in other industries is taken into consideration. The relationship between minimum wages and schooling decisions is more pronounced for young men than for young women.

Throughout this study, the sensitivity of teenage employment to minimum wage regulation and the importance of young persons in the retail labor force have been repeatedly emphasized. It should thus come as no surprise that youths at the age when they must decide whether to begin and continue college are influenced by factors affecting the labor market in an industry that is responsible for much of their employment.

Over the period from 1960 through 1978, school attendance averaged 46 percent of the population of eighteen- and nineteen-year-old males and 39 percent of eighteen- and nineteen-year-old females. The impact of minimum wage regulation on average hourly earnings in retail trade varied from zero in 1960 to as high as 5.5 percent in 1968 (see table 11, column 1). According to the statistical results reported in appendix D, when average retail trade wages were raised by 2.5 percent as the result of minimum wage legislation (about the average over the period 1960–1978), the fraction of eighteen- and nineteen-year-old young men attending school was increased by about

[11] Mattila, "The Impact of Minimum Wages on Teenage Schooling."

0.064, or about 14 percent of the average fraction attending school. That is, almost 6.5 percent—nearly a quarter million individuals—of this group of young men attended school (probably college or junior college) who would not have done so had employment opportunities not been reduced by minimum wage regulation in retail trade. The comparable figure for eighteen- and nineteen-year-old young women is about half as large.

What policy conclusions can be drawn from this relationship? It may be tempting to conclude that at last a beneficial effect of minimum wage legislation has been discovered. Young people are encouraged to acquire some college education and increase their future productivity. But as pointed out above, such a conclusion may not be warranted. The additional schooling acquired is not costless, either to the individuals acquiring it or to society at large. The private and social costs include the labor not performed as these additional school attendees give up their efforts to find full-time market work to attend school as well as the direct expenditures on books, instructors, and the additional construction of lecture halls, classrooms, laboratories, and equipment induced by increased enrollments. These individuals evidently had evaluated their own abilities and talents such that they believed they would benefit more from the earning and training opportunities provided by the labor market than by further formal training in school. That is, weighing their assessment of the benefits of further schooling against only their own private costs—ignoring the additional costs borne by others in the form of taxes to subsidize their attending public colleges and junior colleges—they opted not to acquire further schooling. Only legislative interference in the labor market caused them to choose to continue or reenter school. Thus, the resources devoted to additional schooling are not likely to have been well spent.

Minimum Wage Rates and Training. The impact of minimum wage regulation on the benefits of market work in the form of future wage growth is clearer than the impact on future earning power through additional schooling. Appendix D describes in detail how a major longitudinal survey of young men living in the United States between 1966 and 1971 was used to estimate the impact of minimum wage legislation on the wage gain attributable to on-the-job training over two time periods, 1966–1969 and 1966–1971. Analysis of these data reveals no separate or additional effect of minimum wage legislation in *retail trade* on human capital investment through training, but it does reveal a substantial impact of minimum wage legislation *in general.* This implies that extension of minimum wage coverage to retail trade significantly decreased the ability of young workers to improve their future earning prospects through early work experience, increasing the relative importance of schooling as the only means of improving their economic status. Whether the schools perform this function as efficiently as actual work experience in the absence of minimum wage controls is open to debate, particularly for those individuals who perceive that, for them, work experience is the preferred means of investing in human capital.

The analysis of the effect of minimum wage rates on wage growth and full wage rates was carried out separately for work experience obtained while an individual was attending school and while he was not enrolled. Then, full wage rates were computed for four hypothetical groups of individuals: (1) those who worked in jobs covered by minimum wage legislation in 1966 and who were enrolled in school over the entire period (1966–1969 or 1966–1971); (2) covered workers who were not enrolled at any time; (3) those who worked at jobs not covered by minimum wage legislation in 1966 and were enrolled in school throughout the period; and (4) those whose jobs were not covered and who were not enrolled in school.

As one would expect, the reported wage rates are higher on covered jobs than on jobs not covered by minimum wage regulation—$1.44 per hour for covered youths enrolled in school and $1.93 for those not enrolled, as opposed to $1.24 and $1.53 for their counterparts not "protected" by a legal wage floor. As suggested above, however, when the impact of work experience on future earnings is taken into consideration, the wage advantage of working at a covered job is not only eliminated, it is apparently reversed! The calculations of the on-the-job training component of the full wage were carried out assuming that the average wage increase associated with work experience acquired between 1966 and 1969 or 1971 would last throughout an average individual's remaining working life. The present value of this "annuity" was computed using a 10 percent rate of discount. The on-the-job training component of the full wage of covered workers amounts to $0.14 per hour for experience gained while attending school and $0.25 for experience acquired while not enrolled in school; these amounts for noncovered workers are $2.29 and $2.78, respectively. When these on-the-job training wage components are added to reported wages, full wage rates amount to $1.58 and $2.16 for covered workers in school and out of school, but $3.53 and $4.31 for those not covered.

This reversal of wage inequality between covered and noncovered workers when reported wage rates are compared with full wage rates was not expected and is not predicted by a simple theory of minimum wage rate effects. It is intriguing to speculate why it occurs. One possible explanation, of course, is that there are errors in the economic model used to estimate the relationship between experience, minimum wage rates, and wage growth. Although this explanation cannot be ruled out, our results are so strong that it seems unlikely future research will overturn the conclusion that the training value of early life work experience is significantly reduced by responses to minimum wage legislation. Another explanation is that the reversal of wage inequality is real, but is not caused entirely by the effects of minimum wage rates. Firms covered by minimum wage legislation are relatively large and are the most likely to be subject to other forms of costly regulation as well—for example, health and safety regulation, pension plan regulation, and so on. The costs of complying with all these other forms of regulation may also impinge on the opportunities firms offer for on-the-job training. Whether this is so must be determined by future research.

Appendix A

Further Discussion of Partial Coverage

This appendix contains a rigorous presentation of the relationship between wage and employment changes in the covered and noncovered sectors and the industry average wage and employment change.[1] By assumption all workers disemployed in the covered sector would be willing to work in the noncovered sector at the old free market wage W_0. Thus,

$$\Delta L^c \equiv L_0{}^c - L_1{}^c = \Delta L^n + L_2{}^n - L_1{}^n \qquad \text{(A.1)}$$

where $\Delta L^n \equiv L_1{}^n - L_0{}^n$, $L_0{}^c \equiv$ quantity of labor employed in the covered sector before the imposition of minimum wage legislation, $L_1{}^c \equiv$ quantity of labor employed in the covered sector after the imposition of minimum wage legislation, $L_0{}^n \equiv$ quantity of labor employed in the noncovered sector before the imposition of minimum wage legislation, $L_1{}^n \equiv$ quantity of labor employed in the noncovered sector after the imposition of minimum wage legislation, and $L_2{}^n \equiv$ quantity of labor that would accept employment in the noncovered sector after the imposition of minimum wage legislation at the old free market wage W_0.

Using the equality expressed in (A.1), we can relate wage changes in the covered and noncovered sectors as follows:

$$\eta^c \left(\frac{\Delta W}{W_0}\right)^c L_0{}^c = -\left(\frac{\Delta W}{W_0}\right)^n L_0{}^n \left(\eta_D{}^n - \eta_S{}^n\right) \qquad \text{(A.2)}$$

where $\eta_D{}^c$, $\eta_D{}^n \equiv$ the (arc) elasticities of demand for labor in the covered and noncovered sectors, respectively, $\eta_S{}^n \equiv$ the (arc) elasticity

[1] A simple geometric analysis can be found in Belton M. Fleisher and Thomas J. Kniesner, *Labor Economics: Theory, Evidence, and Policy*, 2nd ed. (Englewood Cliffs, N.J.: Prentice-Hall, 1980), pp. 163-66.

of supply of labor in the noncovered sector, $\Delta W^c \equiv$ the minimum wage W_{MIN} less the free market wage W_0, and $\Delta W^n \equiv$ the change in the wage rate in the noncovered sector.

From (A.2) we can easily derive

$$\frac{\left(\frac{\Delta W}{W_0}\right)^n}{\left(\frac{\Delta W}{W_0}\right)^c} = -\frac{L_0{}^c}{L_0{}^n} \cdot \frac{\eta_D{}^c}{\eta_D{}^n - \eta_S{}^n} \tag{A.3}$$

(A.3) can readily be used to show when the wage decline in the covered sector will be equal in magnitude to the wage increase in the covered sector. The condition is

$$-\frac{L_0{}^c}{L_0{}^n} \cdot \frac{\eta_D{}^c}{\eta_D{}^n - \eta_S{}^n} = -1 \tag{A.4}$$

The industry-wide average wage change is

$$\left(\frac{\Delta \overline{W}}{W_0}\right) = \left(\frac{\Delta W}{W_0}\right)^c \frac{L_0{}^c}{L_0{}^c + L_0{}^n} + \left(\frac{\Delta W}{W_0}\right)^n \frac{L_0{}^n}{L_0{}^c + L_0{}^n} \tag{A.5}$$

By making use of (A.3), we can write (A.5) in terms of ΔW^c alone:

$$\left(\frac{\Delta \overline{W}}{W_0}\right) = \left(\frac{\Delta W}{W_0}\right)^c \left[\frac{L_0{}^c(\eta_D{}^n - \eta_S{}^n - \eta_D{}^c}{(L_0{}^c + L_0{}^n)\ (\eta_D{}^n - \eta_S{}^n)}\right] \tag{A.6}$$

The condition for $\frac{\Delta \overline{W}}{W_0}$ to equal zero when $\left(\frac{\Delta W}{W_0}\right)^c \equiv \frac{W_{MIN} - W_0}{W_0}$ is positive is

$$\eta_D{}^c = \eta_D{}^n - \eta_S{}^n \tag{A.7}$$

The economic meaning of this condition is especially transparent if we assume that no workers ever drop out of the labor force—that is, $\eta_S{}^n = 0$. Then, with incomplete coverage, equal demand elasticities assure that the increased wage in the covered sector is exactly offset by the decline in the noncovered wage multiplied by the ratio of noncovered workers to covered workers. The larger is the noncovered sector relative to the covered sector, the smaller is the decline in the noncovered wage required to absorb the workers displaced by the minimum wage in the covered sector.

Although important changes in employment result from a minimum wage imposed in the covered sector when industry coverage is incomplete, these changes, too, may be obscured in industry aggregate data. Since the change in industry employment, ΔL, is the sum of the increase in employment in the noncovered sector and the decrease in the covered sector, we can write

$$\Delta L = L_0{}^n \eta_D{}^n \left(\frac{\Delta W}{W_0}\right)^n + L_0 \eta_D{}^c \left(\frac{\Delta W}{W_0}\right)^n \qquad \text{(A.8)}$$

Making use of (A.3) and substituting for $\left(\frac{\Delta W}{W_0}\right)^n$, we obtain

$$\Delta L = \left(\frac{\Delta W}{W}\right)^c L_0{}^c \eta_D{}^c \left(1 - \frac{\eta_D{}^n}{\eta_D{}^n - \eta_S{}^n}\right) \qquad \text{(A.9)}$$

An important implication of (A.9) is that, if the elasticity of supply $\eta_S{}^n$ is zero, $\Delta L = 0$. Why? Since displaced employees are willing to work at any price, the wage rate in the noncovered sector will fall sufficiently to assure their employment. Employment declines for the industry as a whole only insofar as workers seek employment in other (noncovered) industries or drop out of the labor force in response to the declining wage rate in the noncovered sector. Another source of employment decline, not reflected in equation (A.9), is a leftward shift in the labor supply curve of the noncovered sector as workers, attracted by the higher minimum wage in the covered sector, seek employment there by joining the pool of unemployed workers.

Appendix B

Estimation of the Impact of Federal Minimum Wage Regulation on the Cost of Labor in Retail Trade

A Model of Wage Rate Determination in the Absence of Federal Minimum Wage Legislation

In order to estimate the hypothetical course of wage rates in retail trade had there been no federal minimum wage rate legislation applicable to the industry, it is necessary to postulate what other important variables would have operated to change wage rates in retail trade relative to what they would have been under unchanging circumstances. The following variables were initially postulated as likely candidates.

$E \equiv$ *The proportionate effect of minimum wages in the rest of the economy.* By causing an excess supply of low-productivity labor outside retail trade, the number of such workers in retail trade may be increased and their rate of pay decreased by minimum wage rates imposed on other industries in the economy. As Jacob Mincer has shown, minimum wage rates may reduce the supply of labor to non-covered firms if workers are sufficiently willing to wait for jobs paying the minimum wage in covered firms.[1] Therefore, we cannot unambiguously infer an expected sign for E.

$P \equiv$ *The proportion of young persons in the population.* Since retail trade is a relatively intensive employer of young workers, and is evidently growing more so over time, an increase in the proportion of young workers in the population (and in the labor force) is likely to cause the average wage of workers in retail trade to be lower than it would otherwise have been.[2] So long as youthful workers are com-

[1] Jacob Mincer, "Unemployment Effects of Minimum Wages," *Journal of Political Economy*, vol. 84, no. 4, part 2 (August 1976), pp. S87-S104.

[2] Richard B. Freeman, "The Effects of Demographic Factors on Age-Earnings Profiles," *Journal of Human Resources*, vol. 14, no. 3 (Summer 1979), pp. 289-318.

plementary to older workers in production, an increase in the proportion of young workers will lower their wage relative to that of older workers, thus lowering the relative average wage of youth-intensive industries. A decline in the relative wage of young workers will induce substitution of young for older workers, increasing the youth intensity of the labor forces in all industries. Relative youth intensities will increase in those industries where substitution of young workers is relatively easy. There is no good evidence pertaining to the elasticity of substitution between younger and older workers in retail trade compared to other industries, however.[3]

$M \equiv$ *The size of the armed forces relative to the population.* During periods of active military involvement, the expansion of the goods-producing industries would be accompanied by an increase in wage rates in those industries relative to the rest of the economy. During periods of wage and price controls, it would not be surprising if wage ceilings were less rigid in military-oriented industries than in retail trade.

$U \equiv$ *The unemployment rate.* This is a measure of the general business conditions. Fluctuations in the demand for output are felt with greater severity in some industries than in others, and the response to a temporary decline in demand in terms of wage rate adjustments and workers laid off will vary among industries according

[3] Finis Welch, "Effects of Cohort Size on Earnings: The Baby Boom Babies' Financial Bust," *Journal of Political Economy*, vol. 87, no. 5, part 2 (October 1979), pp. S65-S98. Under certain circumstances, a uniform increase in the youth intensity of the labor force in all industries will even result in a decline in the average wage of a relatively youth-intensive industry compared with other industries. Let $W_y =$ the wage of young workers, and $W_o =$ the wage of older workers; $O =$ the number of older workers employed, and $Y =$ the number of young workers. Then the average wage rate in a youth-intensive industry relative to another industry is

$$\frac{\dfrac{W_oO+W_ynrY}{O+ry}}{\dfrac{W_oO+W_ynY}{O+y}} \equiv \frac{\overline{W}_y}{\overline{W}_o}$$

where n is the ratio of young workers to older workers in the labor force at any moment in time divided by the ratio in a base period, and $r > 1$ is the ratio of young to older workers in the youth-intensive industry divided by that in the other industry. The effect of an increase in n on the relative average wage in the youth-intensive industry is

$$\frac{d}{dn}\frac{\overline{W}_y}{\overline{W}_o} = \frac{W_oO+W_ynrY}{W_oO+W_ynY} \times \frac{OY(1\text{-}r)}{(O+nrY)^2} + \frac{O+nY}{O+nrY} \times \frac{W_oOW_yY(r-1)}{(W_oO+W_ynY)^2}$$

$$= 0 \text{ so long as } r \neq 1.$$

When $r > 1$, as assumed, the first term is negative and the second positive. The entire expression is negative under plausible conditions.

to differences in seniority arrangements, implicit employer-employee contracts, firm investments in worker training, and collective bargaining agreements. Thus, consideration of the outcome of these conditions may enhance our ability to predict the hypothetical course of retail wage rates in the absence of minimum wage legislation.

$T \equiv$ *The trend of relative productivity growth.* As pointed out in the main text, it is not unlikely that an influence on the course of wage rates in retail trade has been the growth in productivity over time. On the one hand, productivity growth has resulted in increased wage rates paid to workers of given quality. On the other hand, the probably slower rate of productivity growth in retail trade relative to that in goods-producing industries has created pressure to reduce employment of relatively highly paid workers in retail trade compared to goods-producing industries. This trend is likely to have been reinforced by growing education and skills in consumption of retail customers.

The variable E, measuring the proportionate effect of minimum wage legislation on the cost of labor outside retail trade is, of course, not directly observable for reasons given in the text. Thus, indirect measures are required. Two alternative measures of E are used here. The first measure, E_1, represents an attempt to approximate the proportionate effect of minimum wage legislation on labor cost directly. It is derived as follows. The U.S. Department of Labor (DOL) has estimated the proportionate increase in the average wage bill of covered workers that was required to bring all those receiving less than the minimum wage up to the minimum on three dates when the minimum wage was raised: March 1956, September 1961, and September 1963. They have also provided estimates of the proportion of covered employees earning less than the minimum at the time the minimum was imposed or raised: in 1938, 1939, 1945, 1950, 1956, 1963, 1967, 1968, 1974, 1975, and 1976.[4] Casual inspection of the data suggested that the proportionate increase in the average wage bill is proportionate to the increase in the square of the ratio of the new minimum wage to the average manufacturing wage multiplied by the proportion of covered workers earning less than the new minimum wage. (The lower minimum applicable to newly covered workers is ignored.) Since the estimates of the proportionate increase in the wage bill given by DOL are all calculated in the presence of preexisting minimum wages, it is necessary to adjust the DOL estimates upward

[4] U.S. Department of Labor, Bureau of Labor Statistics, "The Fair Labor Standards Act: Changes of Four Decades," *Monthly Labor Review*, vol. 102 (July 1979), pp. 10-16.

for the effect on wage costs of the old minimum. This is accomplished by assuming that, had the \$0.40 minimum prevailed through 1950, the impact on the average wage bill would have been negligible. (The \$0.40 minimum had become effective in 1945, and the average manufacturing wage had risen by 42 percent.) Data on the proportion of covered workers earning less than the minimum for years between increases in the minimum were interpolated, assuming that this proportion is proportionate to the square of the ratio of the minimum to the average wage in manufacturing during the year in question divided by this ratio for the preceding year. In years when a new minimum wage was imposed, E_1 was calculated both with the new minimum and with the old minimum, and a weighted average was calculated, based on the number of months the new minimum was in effect. A more detailed description of this variable is available from the author on request.

The second measure, E_2, is similar to the indirect measures used in many studies of minimum wage rates. It is

$$E_{2t} \equiv \sum_i (M_{it}C_{it})\frac{e_{it}}{T_t} \qquad \text{(B.1)}$$

where

$M_{it} \equiv$ the ratio of the minimum wage rate to the average wage in industry i; $i = 1, \ldots, 7$, represents each major industry group except retail trade and agriculture.

$C_{it} \equiv$ the proportion of nonsupervisory workers employed in firms covered by federal minimum wage legislation.

$e_{it} \equiv$ the number of nonsupervisory employees in industry i.

$T_t \equiv \sum_i e_{it}$.

$t \equiv 1938, 1939, \ldots, 1978.$

The data on coverage are unpublished and furnished by the Employment Standards Administration of the Department of Labor.[5] Wage data are from various issues of the Department of Labor's *Employment and Earnings*, extrapolated where necessary with data on annual earnings of full-time employees published by the U.S. Department of Commerce.[6] In each year, the minimum wage is calculated as an employment-weighted average of the rate applicable to newly covered workers and the minimum applicable to previously covered workers. In years when the minimum was raised, a monthly

[5] I am grateful to John Peterson for providing me with a copy of these data.

[6] U.S. Department of Commerce, Office of Business Economics, *The National Income and Product Accounts of the United States, 1929–65* (1967).

TABLE B1

CALCULATED VALUES OF E_1 AND E_2

Year	E_1 (percent)	E_2	Year	E_1 (percent)	E_2
1938	0.03	0.021	1959	0.65	0.339
1939	0.23	0.144	1960	0.54	0.325
1940	0.47	0.163	1961	0.64	0.329
1941	0.27	0.151	1962	0.85	0.367
1942	0.10	0.134	1963	0.96	0.363
1943	0.03	0.127	1964	1.25	0.361
1944	0.02	0.124	1965	1.07	0.350
1945	0.09	0.165	1966	0.87	0.389
1946	0.32	0.280	1967	1.36	0.401
1947	0.13	0.256	1968	2.58	0.431
1948	0.05	0.233	1969	2.06	0.426
1949	0.02	0.222	1970	1.59	0.410
1950	0.81	0.374	1971	1.16	0.387
1951	0.59	0.368	1972	0.81	0.362
1952	0.45	0.346	1973	0.55	0.338
1953	0.34	0.332	1974	0.35	0.358
1954	0.30	0.318	1975	0.33	0.378
1955	0.23	0.305	1976	0.30	0.385
1956	0.97	0.369	1977	0.18	0.365
1957	0.90	0.368	1978	0.23	0.392
1958	0.77	0.351			

SOURCE: See text.

weighted average of the new and old minimums was computed. Except in 1945, when a particularly sharp change occurred in the proportion of workers covered in all seven industries, C_{it} is not a weighted average of the old and new values within a year; rather the new figure is used in every year when reported coverage changed.

The calculated values of E_1 and E_2 for 1938–1978 are presented in Table B1.

Regression Analysis

The variables described above were incorporated in the following models of wage determination in retail trade:

$$\ln \frac{W_{rt}}{W_{mt}} = \alpha_0 + \alpha_1 \frac{e_{mt}}{e_{rt}} \ln(1 + 0.01E_1) + \alpha_2 \ln P + \alpha_3 \ln M + \alpha_4 \ln U + \alpha_5 T \qquad \text{(B.2)}$$

and

$$\ln \frac{W_{rt}}{W_{mt}} = \alpha_0' + \alpha_1' \frac{e_t}{e_{rt}} E_2 + \alpha_2' \ln P + \alpha_3' \ln M + \alpha_4' \ln U + \alpha_5' T \quad \text{(B.3)}$$

The exact definition of the variables in equations (B.2) and (B.3) and the data sources from which they were obtained are:

$W_{rt} \equiv$ average hourly earnings of nonsupervisory workers in retail trade (excluding workers in eating and drinking establishments). Source: U.S. Department of Labor, Bureau of Labor Statistics, *Employment and Earnings, United States.*[7]

$W_{mt} \equiv$ average hourly earnings of production workers in durable goods manufacturing. This variable is included to represent variables affecting productivity and wage rates not captured by the other variables included in the models. The average wage in durable goods manufacturing, being higher than in all manufacturing, is less likely to be directly influenced by the minimum wage legislation represented by E_1 and E_2. Source: same as W_{rt}.

$e_{mt}, e_{rt} \equiv$ employment in manufacturing and retail trade, respectively. During the early years of federal minimum wage legislation, manufacturing workers represent the largest group covered. "Normalizing" the minimum wage variable with the ratio e_{mt}/e_{rt} implies that $\alpha_1 = \eta_{DM}/(\eta_{DR} - \eta_{SR})$, where η_{DM} and η_{DR} are the elasticities of demand for labor in manufacturing and retail trade, respectively, and η_{SR} is the elasticity of supply of labor to retail trade. See appendix A.

$e_t \equiv$ total nonfarm employment except retail trade. Source of e variables: U.S. Department of Labor, Bureau of Labor Statistics, *Employment and Earnings, United States* (various issues).

$P \equiv$ population age 15–24 $\div$ population age 15–64. Sources: U.S. Bureau of the Census, *Historical Sta-*

[7] Data for years before 1939 are extrapolated on the basis of the equation $\ln W_{rt} = -7.95962 + 1.01709\, W_{rt}^*$, where W_{rt}^* = average annual earnings of full-time employees in retail trade, $t = 1939, \ldots, 1961$. See U.S. Department of Commerce, Office of Business Economics, *The National Income and Product Accounts of the United States, 1929–65,* statistical tables.

tistics of the United States, Colonial Times to 1970, Series A29–42 (1975); after 1970, U.S. Bureau of the Census, *Current Population Reports,* Series P-25, no. 72 (April 1978).

$M \equiv$ the number of military personnel ÷ population age 15–64. Sources: *Historical Statistics of the United States,* Series A29–42 and Y904–916; after 1970, U.S. Bureau of the Census, *Statistical Abstract of the United States, 1979* (1979) and *Current Population Reports,* Series P-25.

$U \equiv$ civilian labor force unemployment rate in percent. Source: *Historical Statistics of the United States* and U.S. Department of Labor, *Employment and Training Report of the President, 1979* (1980).

$T \equiv$ a trend variable equal to 1 for the first year of a series of observations, 2 in the second year, and so on.

Equations (B.2) and (B.3) were estimated over two time periods, both of which ended in the year federal minimum wage legislation was imposed on the retail trade industry, 1932–1961 and 1936–1961. The longer time period has the advantage of including years during which the dependent variable exhibited a particularly sharp decline, and thus might provide a better estimate of a long-term tendency for retail trade wage rates to decline relative to wage rates in goods-producing industries. Available measures of the average retail trade wage rate, however, require piecing together two different time series to obtain data before 1939, possibly contributing additional error to the longer series. The ordinary least squares (OLS) estimates for each time period exhibited positive serial correlation, but those based on the longer period had much lower Durbin-Watson statistics. Even after correction for serial correlation, the regressions based on the shorter time period appeared to be better predictors of the later observations than those based on the longer period. For example, the sum of the absolute values of the last five residuals is about twice as large in the regressions based on the 1932–1961 period as in those based on 1936–1961. Since we are particularly interested in extrapolating the regression results into the post-1961 period, the regression results based on the years 1936–1961 appear to be better for our purposes.

The coefficient of the unemployment variable never approaches statistical significance in the estimates, so only results excluding this variable are presented here. The regressions using E_1 yielded consistently higher R^2 than those using E_2, and this seems a sufficiently good

TABLE B2

ESTIMATES OF THE RETAIL WAGE EQUATION, 1936–1961
(t-ratios and asymptotic t-ratios in parentheses)[a]

Row	$\frac{e_{mt}}{e_{rt}}\ln(1+0.01E_1)$	$\ln P$	$\ln M$	T	*Durbin-Watson*	*Rho (final iteration)*
			OLS Estimates			
1	−1.41	−0.477	−0.0594	−0.00183	0.89	—
	(0.9)	(2.7)	(7.7)	(0.8)		
2	−1.86	−0.363	−0.0609		0.91	—
	(1.3)	(3.3)	(8.1)			
			GLS Estimates			
3	−0.429	−0.412	−0.0581	−0.00228	1.54	0.51
	(0.4)	(1.8)	(6.3)	(0.9)		
4	−0.664	−0.254	−0.0597		1.54	0.51
	(0.6)	(1.8)	(6.5)			

[a] Asymptotic t-ratios based on twenty-six degrees of freedom.

criterion for choosing E_1 over E_2 as an appropriate measure of the impact of minimum wage legislation outside retail trade.

Regression results using E_1 are shown in table B2. The bottom half of the table contains generalized least squares (GLS) estimates corrected for first-order autocorrelation of residuals using a Cochrane-Orcutt type iterative least-squares procedure.[8] The coefficient of the trend variable, T_1, is statistically insignificant and quantitatively very small. The coefficient of the military variable is statistically significant and quite insensitive to the inclusion of the trend variable and correction for autocorrelation. The coefficient of the proportion of young workers is negative as expected. Its magnitude and t-value fall when the estimates are corrected for autocorrelation, but the t-value remains high enough to warrant concluding that, when the proportion of young people in the population rises, the average wage of retail trade employees declines.

The coefficient of the E_1 variable is sensitive both to the inclusion of the trend variable and to correction for autocorrelation. On the basis of these regressions, as well as those in which E_2 is used (not

[8] Kenneth J. White, *Shazam: An Econometrics Computer Program,* Version 2.0 (Houston: Rice University, Department of Economics, September 1977), p. 44.

reported here), I conclude that federal minimum wage legislation applied to other industries did not significantly depress the average wage rate in retail trade.[9] This negative result is of considerable importance because, as we have seen, it suggests that the principal impact of minimum wage legislation is on employment, unemployment, and/or labor force participation.

The Hypothetical Path of the Retail Trade Average Wage, 1962–1977

On the basis of the four estimates of the retail wage equation reported in table B2, six different forecasts of the average wage rate in retail trade may be derived, two based on the OLS estimates and four based on the GLS estimates. Forecast values of W_{rt} can be obtained from the GLS estimates based only on the estimated regression coefficients as well as by incorporating the information obtained regarding the autoregressive process generating the disturbances of the wage relationship. The latter are BLU estimates.[10] These forecasts (W_{rt}^*) are reported in table B3, along with the observed values of W_{rt} for $t =$ 1962, . . . , 1978. Several features of W_{rt}^* bear commenting upon: (1) W_{rt}^*, the forecast value, is always less than W_{rt}; (2) $W_{rt}—W_{rt}^*$ is by no means constant, generally increasing through the late 1960s, and then diminishing; (3) the magnitude of $W_{rt}—W_{rt}^*$ also varies considerably among the various specifications of the wage equations.

Table B4 facilitates examination of the variation in the deviation of forecasted from observed retail wage rates by presenting calculations in proportionate form, $(W_{rt}—W_{rt}^*) \div W_{rt}^*$. Clearly, the deviations are smallest when the forecasts incorporate information on the autocorrelated error term of the estimated wage relationships. These are the BLU estimates reported in table B4. Even these values for $(W_{rt}—W_{rt}^*) \div W_{rt}^*$ are large by comparison with estimates of the impact of minimum wage legislation on labor costs in retail trade. The 2.5 percent confidence interval on the positive side of W_{rt}^* is shown for the row 4 BLU forecast in the last column of table B4, expressed as $(W_{rt}—W_{rt}^*) \div W_{rt}^*$. This is the forecast wage on which further

[9] Mincer claims that "empirical analysis suggests . . . wages in the uncovered sector fall," but reports no estimates of this empirical relationship; see Mincer, "Unemployment Effects of Minimum Wages." Tauchen obtains inconsistent results for the relationship between agricultural wage rates and minimum wages in nonfarm industries; see George E. Tauchen, "Some Empirical Evidence on Cross-Sector Effects of the Minimum Wage" (unpublished paper, July 1978, drawn from Ph.D. diss., University of Minnesota, 1978).

[10] Arthur Goldberger, "Best Linear Unbiased Prediction in a Linear Regression Model," *Journal of the American Statistical Association*, vol. 57 (June 1962), pp. 369-75.

TABLE B3

FORECAST AND OBSERVED VALUES OF W_{rt}, 1962–1978

Year	*Observed Values* (W_{rt})	*Forecast Values Based on Estimated Relationships of Table B2* (W_{rt}*)					
		Row 1	Row 2	Row 3	Row 4	Row 3 BLU[a]	Row 4 BLU[a]
1962	1.74	1.63	1.67	1.64	1.69	1.66	1.69
1963	1.80	1.64	1.69	1.66	1.73	1.68	1.73
1964	1.87	1.66	1.71	1.69	1.76	1.70	1.76
1965	1.96	1.69	1.76	1.72	1.81	1.73	1.81
1966	2.04	1.73	1.81	1.76	1.86	1.76	1.86
1967	2.17	1.74	1.82	1.78	1.90	1.79	1.90
1968	2.33	1.78	1.85	1.86	1.98	1.87	1.98
1969	2.48	1.90	1.99	1.97	2.11	1.97	2.11
1970	2.64	2.02	2.13	2.08	2.24	2.08	2.24
1971	2.78	2.18	2.32	2.22	2.41	2.22	2.41
1972	2.94	2.38	2.54	2.41	2.62	2.41	2.62
1973	3.13	2.56	2.75	2.58	2.82	2.58	2.82
1974	3.38	2.78	3.00	2.79	3.06	2.80	3.06
1975	3.65	3.05	3.29	3.06	3.36	3.06	3.36
1976	3.90	3.30	3.57	3.30	3.64	3.31	3.64
1977	4.20	3.59	3.89	3.59	3.96	3.59	3.96
1978	4.61	3.94	4.26	3.93	4.34	3.94	4.34

[a] For explanation of BLU estimates, see text.

work is based, and only the positive half of the confidence interval is shown because $W_{rt}—W_{rt}^*$ is always positive for $t = 1962, \ldots, 1978$.[11]

Table B5 contains calculations showing which variables in the estimated wage relationships are doing the "work" in generating W_{rt}^*. Each column of table B5 shows the product of a regression coefficient and its respective variable in a given year, divided by the corresponding product in 1961. (The coefficient of W_{mt} was constrained to equal unity.) Calculations are shown for all the estimates reported in table B2. The product of all these calculations across a row for each individual wage relationship yields the ratio $W_{rt}^* \div W_{r1961}^*$. For example, the product for the relationship reported in table B2, row 1, in 1969 is $1.357 \times 0.965 \times 0.909 \times 0.988 \times 0.985 = 1.158$. If W_{rt} had grown at the same rate as W_{mt}, it would have been 35.7 percent

[11] I am grateful to Mark Berger for computing this confidence interval for me. See Goldberger, "Best Linear Unbiased Prediction."

TABLE B4

PROPORTIONATE DEVIATION OF FORECAST VALUE (W_{rt}^*) FROM OBSERVED VALUES OF W_{rt}: $(W_{rt} - W_{rt}^*) \div W_{rt}^*$

	Forecast Values Based on Table B2						
						Row 4 BLU	
Year	Row 1	Row 2	Row 3	Row 4	Row 3 BLU	Fore-cast	2.5 percent confidence interval[a]
1962	0.067	0.042	0.061	0.030	0.047	0.028	0.067
1963	0.098	0.065	0.084	0.040	0.071	0.041	0.070
1964	0.127	0.094	0.107	0.063	0.103	0.060	0.084
1965	0.160	0.114	0.140	0.083	0.135	0.082	0.083
1966	0.179	0.127	0.159	0.097	0.158	0.096	0.083
1967	0.247	0.192	0.219	0.142	0.214	0.144	0.105
1968	0.309	0.259	0.253	0.177	0.247	0.177	0.159
1969	0.305	0.246	0.259	0.175	0.256	0.177	0.137
1970	0.307	0.239	0.269	0.179	0.269	0.180	0.117
1971	0.275	0.198	0.252	0.154	0.257	0.153	0.104
1972	0.235	0.157	0.220	0.122	0.218	0.120	0.093
1973	0.223	0.138	0.213	0.110	0.211	0.110	0.088
1974	0.216	0.127	0.211	0.105	0.208	0.104	0.085
1975	0.197	0.109	0.193	0.086	0.191	0.085	0.084
1976	0.182	0.092	0.182	0.071	0.179	0.071	0.084
1977	0.170	0.080	0.170	0.061	0.168	0.060	0.081
1978	0.170	0.082	0.173	0.062	0.170	0.062	0.080

[a] See text.

greater in 1969 than in 1961. Based on past behavior, however, the wage relationship predicts that, had no minimum wage rate been in effect in retail trade, the average wage in the industry would not have grown as rapidly as in durable goods manufacturing. Why? The impact of minimum wage rates outside retail trade would have lowered retail trade wages by 3.5 percent relative to wage rates in durable manufacturing. The labor market impact of the "baby boom" generation would have added a further 9.1 percent reduction, the Vietnam war as measured by the relative size of the military a reduction of 1.2 percent, and trend still another 1.5 percent. The relationships without the trend variable generally show a smaller negative impact of the minimum wage rate outside retail trade and of the proportion of young persons in the population on the retail trade wage rate. Thus, since

TABLE B5

CONTRIBUTION OF $(e_{mt}/e_{rt})\ \ln(1+0.01E_1)$, P, M, AND T TO $W_{rt}^* \div W_{r\,1961}^*$ [a]

		Forecast Values Based on Table B2													
		Row 1				Row 2			Row 3				Row 4		
Year	$\frac{W_{mt}}{W_{m\,1961}}$	E[b]	P	M	T	E[b]	P	M	E[b]	P	M	T	E[b]	P	M
1962	1.028	0.994	0.979	0.994	0.998	0.992	0.984	0.994	0.998	0.982	0.994	0.998	0.997	0.989	0.994
1963	1.056	0.991	0.964	0.997	0.996	0.988	0.972	0.997	0.997	0.969	0.997	0.995	0.996	0.981	0.997
1964	1.088	0.984	0.951	0.998	0.995	0.979	0.962	0.998	0.995	0.958	0.998	0.993	0.992	0.974	0.998
1965	1.121	0.989	0.934	1.000	0.993	0.985	0.954	1.000	0.997	0.947	1.000	0.991	0.994	0.967	1.000
1966	1.165	0.994	0.929	0.992	0.991	0.992	0.946	0.992	0.998	0.939	0.992	0.989	0.997	0.962	0.992
1967	1.205	0.981	0.921	0.988	0.989	0.975	0.939	0.988	0.994	0.931	0.988	0.986	0.991	0.957	0.988
1968	1.281	0.951	0.917	0.986	0.987	0.936	0.936	0.986	0.985	0.927	0.986	0.984	0.977	0.955	0.986
1969	1.357	0.965	0.909	0.988	0.985	0.955	0.930	0.988	0.989	0.921	0.989	0.982	0.984	0.951	0.988
1970	1.426	0.980	0.902	0.997	0.984	0.973	0.924	0.996	0.994	0.914	0.997	0.980	0.990	0.946	0.997
1971	1.522	0.991	0.894	1.005	0.982	0.989	0.918	1.005	0.997	0.907	1.005	0.977	0.996	0.942	1.005
1972	1.631	1.000	0.896	1.015	0.980	0.999	0.920	1.016	1.000	0.910	1.015	0.975	1.000	0.943	1.015
1973	1.743	1.005	0.896	1.018	0.978	1.007	0.920	1.018	1.002	0.909	1.018	0.973	1.003	0.943	1.018
1974	1.884	1.010	0.895	1.021	0.976	1.013	0.919	1.022	1.003	0.909	1.021	0.971	1.005	0.943	1.022
1975	2.064	1.010	0.894	1.023	0.975	1.015	0.919	1.024	1.003	0.908	1.023	0.969	1.005	0.942	1.023
1976	2.223	1.012	0.894	1.026	0.973	1.016	0.919	1.026	1.004	0.908	1.025	0.966	1.006	0.942	1.026
1977	2.418	1.014	0.897	1.027	0.971	1.019	0.920	1.027	1.004	0.910	1.026	0.964	1.007	0.944	1.027
1978	2.643	1.013	0.900	1.028	0.969	1.017	0.923	1.029	1.004	0.913	1.027	0.962	1.006	0.945	1.028

[a] Each entry is the product of a regression coefficient and its respective variable in the year indicated divided by the corresponding product in 1961.

[b] $E \equiv \frac{e_{mt}}{e_{rt}} \ln(1+0.01E_1)$.

trend (T) has a negative coefficient, the relationships that include trend tend always to yield a larger value of $W_{rt}—W_{rt}^*$ than the relationships without it, and this difference becomes larger over time.

Because the coefficient of T does not attain statistical significance either before or after correction for serial correlation, and also because the error in estimating W_{rt}^* grows as the deviation of the independent variables in the forecasting equation from their mean values increases, it appears best to rely on the wage relationship from which trend has been excluded. Thus, the values of W_{rt}^* upon which we base further discussion of the impact of minimum wage legislation on the average wage rate in retail trade are the BLU forecasts generated by the estimated wage relationship reported in row 4 of table B2. Once again, these forecasts may be found in the last column of table B3, and the proportionate deviation of the observed mean wage in retail trade from these forecast values, along with the 2.5 percent confidence interval for positive deviations, are reported in the last two columns of table B4.

The Effect of Minimum Wage Rates on the Mean Wage Rate in Retail Trade

One purpose of estimating the course of the mean wage in retail trade had there been no federal minimum wage legislation applicable to the industry is to derive an estimate of the proportionate increase in the mean wage that would result if all workers earning less than the minimum were brought up to that level. This calculation requires knowledge not only of the mean wage in the absence of a wage floor, but also of the frequency distribution of wage rates below the minimum. Once a minimum wage has been imposed, the same problems that prevent us from observing the mean wage directly also stand in the way of obtaining information on the frequency distribution.

The procedure used to circumvent this problem is made possible by the existence of a detailed survey of wage rates in retail trade conducted by the U.S. Bureau of Labor Statistics (BLS) in 1956, just a few years before federal minimum wage legislation was imposed.[12] By assuming that the relevant portion of the frequency distribution of retail trade wage rates relative to the mean wage $f(W_r/\overline{W}_r)$ is stable over time, it is possible to use information from the 1956 BLS study to estimate the frequency distribution that would have been observed in any year after 1961 had no minimum wage been in effect.

[12] U.S. Department of Labor, Bureau of Labor Statistics, *Employee Earnings in Retail Trade in October 1956* (July 1957).

FIGURE B1

FREQUENCY DISTRIBUTION OF WAGE RATES IN RETAIL TRADE, OCTOBER 1956

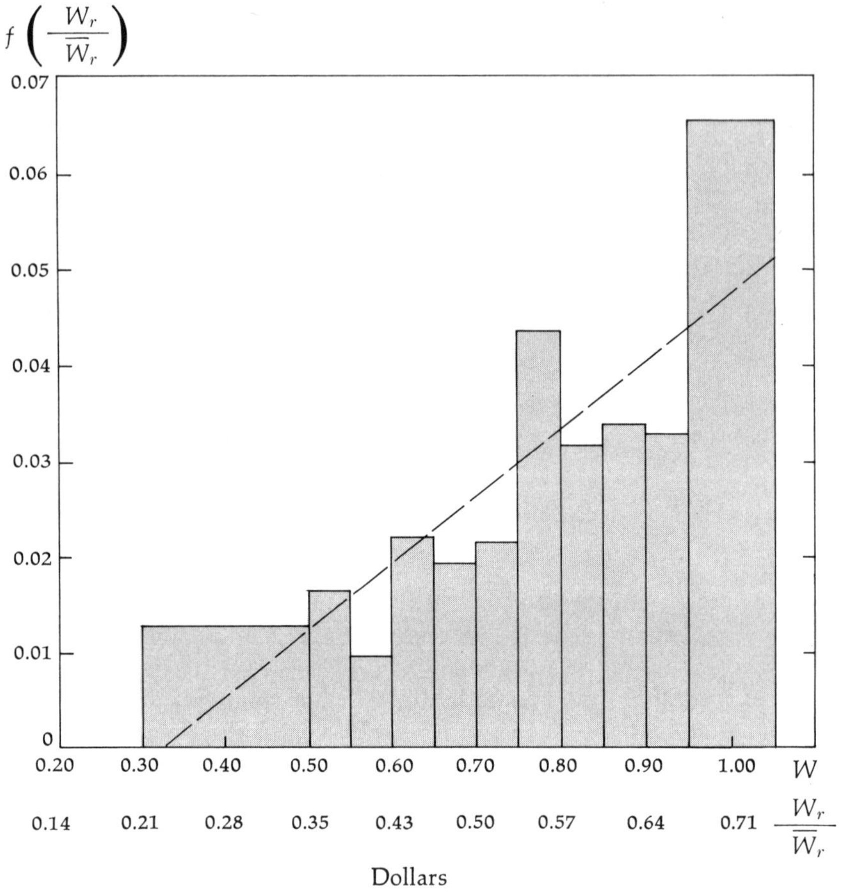

SOURCE: U.S. Department of Labor, Bureau of Labor Statistics, *Employee Earnings in Retail Trade in October 1956*, Bulletin No. 1220, July 1957.

Figure B1 shows a histogram of the frequency distribution of straight-time average hourly earnings relative to the mean wage of nonsupervisory employees in retail trade up to the modal value. A linear function was fit to the midpoints of the histogram by means of OLS regression. The estimated equation,

$$f\left(\frac{W_r}{\overline{W}_r}\right) = \underset{(2.8)}{-0.0281} + \underset{(5.8)}{0.108}\,\frac{W_r}{\overline{W}} \tag{B.4}$$

$\overline{R}^2 = .71$ (t-values in parentheses)

is represented by the broken line in figure B1. The area under this fitted frequency distribution is proportional to an estimate of the fraction of workers receiving less than a given wage, as measured on the horizontal axis. We assume equation (B.4) is unchanging over time and carry out the necessary calculation to estimate the impact of a minimum wage on the average wage paid to covered workers, making use of the estimated mean wage rates described in the last section. Using equation (B.4), we calculate

$$\frac{\Delta W_r^*}{W_r^*} \equiv F\left(\frac{M_r}{\overline{W}_r^*}\right)\frac{M_r}{\overline{W}_r^*} - \int_0^{M_r/\overline{W}_r} f\left(\frac{W_r}{\overline{W}_r^*}\right)\frac{W_r}{\overline{W}_r^*}\, d\,\frac{W_r}{\overline{W}_r^*} \qquad \text{(B.5)}$$

where $F(\bullet) \equiv \int_0^{M_r/\overline{W}_r^*} f(\bullet)\, d\frac{W_r}{\overline{W}_r^*}$

M_r is the minimum wage in retail trade; $f(\bullet)$ is obtained from equation (B.4); and $\overline{W}_r^*$ is the forecast wage in retail trade. The variable $\Delta W_r^*/W_r^*$ is the proportionate increase in the mean wage that would result if all subminimum workers were paid the minimum wage.

In calculating $\Delta W_r^*/W_r^*$, the following adjustments were made to account for differential minimum wage rates within retail trade for newly covered workers and for years during which the minimum was raised: First, $\Delta W_r^*/W_r^*$ was calculated twice—once using the minimum wage applicable to newly covered workers, and once with the minimum wage applicable to previously covered workers—and a weighted sum was constructed. The weights were the number of workers covered by the respective minimum wage rates divided by the total number of covered workers. Second, during years in which M_r takes on two values because of a change in the minimum wage and/or coverage, two values of $\Delta W_r^*/W_r^*$ were calculated, one for each part of the year. Then the two values were weighted by the fraction of the year each was in effect and summed.

The Impact of Federal Minimum Wage Legislation on Wage Supplements in Retail Trade

The preceding discussion deals only with direct wage payments to employees. An obvious possible effect, however, of requiring firms to pay a minimum wage is that supplemental wage payments (insurance, pension contributions, and the like) may be reduced. If wage supplements were reduced sufficiently, then there would be no net increase in labor cost to the firm, and disemployment would be less likely to result. It is plausible that minimum wage legislation induces firms to reduce supplemental wage payments to low-wage workers. They can be treated differently from workers whose pay exceeds the wage floor by making eligibility for full or even partial participation in firm-financed pension and health plans depend on having sufficient tenure with the firm so that the unregulated rate of pay of participants would exceed the minimum wage. Another means of discrimination among employees would be to make full eligibility available only to full-time employees. A combination criterion of tenure and weekly hours of work would also be possible. It is worth noting that, if firms find it attractive to offset minimum wage rates by restricting the eligibility of part-time employees in pension and health plans, they will also have an incentive to substitute low-wage employees working short hours for those working longer hours. (This kind of substitution may also occur as a result of any wage increase—attributable to minimum wage legislation or not—as employers attempt to economize on variable labor costs.)[13] Thus, the number of low-wage workers may grow as average weekly hours are reduced, although we would not expect the proportionate growth in the number of workers to exceed the proportionate decline in average weekly hours of work.

In order to measure the relationship between minimum wage rates and supplemental wage payments, the following equations were estimated:

$$S_{rt} = \alpha_0 + \alpha_1 \frac{\Delta W_{rt}^*}{W_{rt}^*} + \alpha_2 T \qquad \text{(B.6)}$$

and

$$S_t = \beta_0 + \beta_1 \frac{E_{1t}}{100} + \beta_2 T \qquad \text{(B.7)}$$

where S_{rt}, $S_t \equiv$ the ratio of annual wage supplements to annual ordinary wages in retail trade and in all industries, respectively.[14] The other variables are defined above. The estimates of equations (B.6) and (B.7) are shown in table B6. The estimated coefficients α_1 and β_1 do imply that wage supplements have been reduced as a result of minimum wage legislation, although the rather low asymptotic t-ratios (especially in conjunction with rather low Durbin-Watson statistics)

[13] M. Ishaq Nadiri and Sherwin Rosen, *A Disequilibrium Model of Demand for Factors of Production*, National Bureau of Economic Research General Series no. 99 (New York: National Bureau of Economic Research, 1973), chapter 2.

[14] Sources of data are U.S. Department of Commerce, *Survey of Current Business* and unpublished data; also U.S. Bureau of the Census, *Historical Statistics of the United States, Colonial Times to 1970* (1975).

TABLE B6

GLS Estimates of the Wage Supplement Equations
(asymptotic *t*-ratios in parentheses)[a]

Equation	Mean Dependent Variable	$\frac{\Delta W_{rt}^*}{W_{rt}^*}$	$\frac{E_{1t}}{100}$	T	Durbin-Watson	Rho (final iteration)
			1948–1978			
B.6	0.076	−0.12 (1.3)		0.0037 (11.0)	1.4	0.91
B.7	0.098		−0.22 (1.5)	0.0047 (10.3)	0.98	0.97
			1960–1978			
B.6	0.097	−0.15 (1.6)		0.0044 (10.2)	1.4	0.84
B.7	0.122		−0.34 (1.8)	0.0053 (8.5)	1.2	0.94

[a] Degrees of freedom = number of observations.

imply that the estimates are not precise. In retail trade, imposition of a minimum wage that would cause $\Delta W_{rt}^*/W_{rt}^*$ to rise by one percentage point is associated with a reduction in the ratio of supplemental wage payments to ordinary wage payments of somewhat more than 0.1 but less than 0.2 percentage points, or about 1.5 percent of the wage supplement ratio. Thus, at the mean value of $\Delta W_{rt}^*/W_{rt}^*$ over the period since minimum wage rates were first imposed on the retail trade industry, the wage supplement ratio has been reduced by about 4 percent of its mean value—not a very large amount even if marginally statistically significant. The comparable magnitude for all industries is smaller by one third to one half, as one might expect given the relatively low wage position of the retail trade industry.

Appendix C

The Impact of Federal Minimum Wage Regulation on Employment and Hours of Work in Retail Trade

Two basic approaches have been adopted to measure the impact of federal minimum wage regulation on employment and hours of work in retail trade. The first approach involves a procedure common to most studies of minimum wage effects—correlating measures of employment or hours of work with one or more measures of the minimum wage relative to, say, the mean industry wage and other variables. The hypothesis tested is that the correlation between the employment and minimum wage variables is negative. The second approach involves measuring the impact of the minimum wage in a more rigorously formulated factor demand framework. The advantage of the second approach is that the quantitative measure of minimum wage employment effects can be evaluated in terms of the parameters of factor demand equations. Such estimates of minimum wage employment effects are appealing because they can easily be evaluated for plausibility through comparison with other empirical studies of factor demand and because the magnitudes of the estimates would be expected to differ over time only insofar as the structure of factor demand relationships changes—presumably a relatively slow process.

Correlating Employment, Hours, and Minimum Wage Rates

The first approach involves estimating the following relationships:

$$\ln\left(\frac{e_{rt}}{pop_t}\right) = \alpha_0 + \alpha_1 \frac{M_{rt}}{W_{rt}} \cdot C + \alpha_2 U_{mt} + \alpha_3 T \qquad \text{(C.1a)}$$

$$\ln\left(\frac{e_{rt}}{pop_t}\right) = \alpha_0' + \alpha_1' \frac{\Delta W_{rt}^*}{W_{rt}^*} + \alpha_2' U_{mt} + \alpha_3' T \qquad \text{(C.1b)}$$

where

$e_{rt} \equiv$ either the number of nonsupervisory employees in retail trade in year t or the number of employees multiplied by average weekly hours of work (total hours). Source of all data: appendix B, except as noted below.

$pop_t \equiv$ the population of the United States in year t.

$M_{rt} \equiv$ the average minimum wage rate in retail trade.

$W_{rt} \equiv$ mean average hourly earnings of nonsupervisory workers in retail trade in year t.

$\Delta W_{rt}^* / W_{rt}^* \equiv$ the proportionate increase in the forecast wage required to bring all workers at least to the minimum wage.

$C \equiv$ the fraction of nonsupervisory employees in covered retail establishments.

$U_{mt} \equiv$ the unemployment rate of men ages thirty-five to fifty-four in year t. Source: U.S. Department of Labor, Bureau of Labor Statistics, *Handbook of Labor Statistics, 1978* (1979); and U.S. Department of Labor, *Employment and Training Report of the President, 1979* (1980).

$T \equiv$ a trend variable equal to 1 in the first year of a series of observations, 2 in the second year, and so on.

We would expect α_1 and α_1' to be negative, indicating that the minimum wage rate reduces employment, other things being equal. We would also expect α_2 and α_2', representing business fluctuations, to be negative, and the trend variable represents an attempt to hold constant other factors exerting a systematic influence on per capita employment and total hours of work. We would expect the estimate of α_1', the coefficient of the more direct measure of the influence of minimum wage rates on labor cost, to be larger relative to its asymptotic standard error than the estimate of α_1.

Equations (C.1a) and (C.1b) were estimated by the same GLS procedure that was used to estimate equations (B.3) and (B.4), the retail wage equations of chapter 2 and appendix B. The results are shown in table C1. The coefficient of the less direct measure of the influence of minimum wage regulation on labor cost, $M_{rt}/W_{rt} \cdot C$, is negative, consistent with our hypothesis, as is the coefficient of the direct measure, $\Delta W_{rt}^*/W_{rt}^*$. While the estimated value of α_1 is always significantly negative, rather than weakly negative, α_1' is more significant than α_1 when the dependent variable is total hours per capita. The interpretation of the estimated coefficient of $\Delta W_{rt}^*/W_{rt}^*$ is as

TABLE C1

GLS ESTIMATES OF EMPLOYMENT AND HOURS EQUATIONS (C.1a) AND (C.1b), 1960–1978

(absolute values of asymptotic t-ratios in parentheses)[a]

Row	$\frac{M_{rt}}{W_{rt}} \cdot C$	$\frac{\Delta W_{rt}^*}{W_{rt}^*}$	U_{mt}	T	Durbin-Watson	Rho (final iteration)
	Dependent Variable per Capita Employment					
1	−0.24		−1.57	0.018	1.5	0.79
	(3.1)		(4.7)	(8.4)		
2		−0.87	−1.48	0.014	1.5	0.67
		(2.5)	(3.9)	(12.2)		
	Dependent Variable per Capita Total Hours					
3	−0.33		−1.21	0.012	1.9	0.54
	(4.0)		(3.3)	(6.1)		
4		−1.50	−1.36	0.0059	1.7	0.28
		(5.0)	(3.7)	(10.5)		

[a] Based on nineteen degrees of freedom.

follows: α_1' is the derivative of the logarithm of employment or total hours per capita with respect to the proportionate effect on average hourly earnings of paying all workers at least the minimum wage. Therefore, the estimates of α_1' imply that a 1 percent increase in average hourly earnings directly caused by minimum wage regulation induces a 0.87 percent decline in retail trade employment per capita and a 1.5 percent decline in total hours of work per capita. These are reasonable magnitudes compared with the information available on the elasticity of demand for labor in retail trade.[1] These estimates also imply that average hours of work per employee fall by 1.5—0.87 = 0.63 percent under the same circumstances.

The Consumer's Demand for Retail Labor

The second approach to estimating the impact of minimum wage legislation on retail employment and hours of work is grounded in the household production framework sketched out in chapter 1. The de-

[1] Philip Glenn Cotterill, "A Model of Labor in Retail Trade" (Ph.D. diss., Northwestern University, 1969).

mand for retail employment is derived ultimately from consumers' demand for retail services. The basic formulation of this model is

$$\ln \frac{e_{rt}}{pop_t} = \alpha_0 + \alpha_1 \ln \frac{Y_t}{pop_t} + \alpha_2 \ln \frac{W_{rt}^* + \Delta W_{rt}^*}{\Pi_{rt}} + \alpha_3 \ln \frac{\Pi_{wt}}{\Pi_{rt}} + \alpha_4 T \quad \text{(C.2)}$$

where $Y_t \equiv$ disposable personal income deflated by the Consumer Price Index; $\Pi_{rt} \equiv$ the GNP deflator for consumer durable and nondurable sales;[2] $\Pi_{wt} \equiv$ an index of the retailers' cost of goods. More precisely, $\Pi_{wt} = 1-$(national income originating in retail trade/total retail sales) $\times\ \Pi_{rt}$. Since national income represents factor payments, and amounts to about 80 percent of gross retail margin (based on conversations with the U.S. Department of Commerce, Bureau of Economic Analysis), Π_{wt} is a close approximation of the average price paid by retailers for the goods they sell. All the other variables were defined in the preceding section.

Equation (C.2) represents a view of the household combining retail workers' services and goods to produce consumption commodities. The variable T is included to reflect omitted factor prices such as the services of capital; α_1 is the income elasticity of derived demand for the services of retail labor. If, as seems likely, the income elasticity of demand for retail services is in the neighborhood of unity, α_1 should also be approximately unity if the production function for retail services is constant returns to scale. (The simple elasticity of deflated per capita retail sales with respect to real per capita income is 0.87 over the period 1947–1978.) The second variable is an instrument for the price of retail labor deflated by the price of retail "productions." The numerator measures labor cost, including the impact of the minimum wage, without being influenced by firms' demand for labor. It is the forecast wage inflated by the dollar impact on average hourly earnings required to pay all covered workers at least the minimum wage (see appendix B). While the ideal deflator (Π) would reflect only "pure" inflation and would not be influenced by the demand for retail service, such an ideal index is unobservable. The third variable measures the deflated price of retail goods (as opposed to retail service). Because of the biases introduced by using a deflator for equation (C.2) that may be influenced by the demand for labor,

[2] The variable Π_{rt} is derived from series F245–271 and E1–22 of U.S. Bureau of the Census, *Historical Statistics of the United States, Colonial Times to 1970* (1975) and the corresponding data in U.S. Bureau of the Census, *Statistical Abstract of the United States, 1979* (1979), tables 1465 and 781, by calculating

$$\text{(dollar values of retail sales)} \div \left(\frac{\text{nondurable sales}}{\text{nondurable deflator}} + \frac{\text{durable sales}}{\text{durable deflator}} \right)$$

and by possible feedback from the wage variable to the demand for retail services, it is probably safer to estimate the relative factor demand equation

$$\ln \frac{e_{rt}}{S_{rt}/\Pi_{rt}} = \beta_0 + \beta_1 \ln \frac{W_{rt}^* + \Delta W_{rt}^*}{\Pi_{wt}} + \beta_2 T \tag{C.3}$$

Equation (C.3) also reflects the view that retail goods and labor are both inputs used by households in the production of consumption commodities. Thus β_1 is an estimate of the elasticity of substitution between retail labor and goods in household production. The data sources for retail sales are the same as for Π_{rt}.

The GLS estimates of equations (C.2) and (C.3) are shown in table C2 for two time periods, 1947–1978 and 1960–1978. The first time period uses all of the data available when the estimation was carried out, and it has the advantage of larger variation in the independent variables than the shorter period. The 1960–1978 period is of interest because it begins one year before the imposition of federal minimum wage rates in the retail trade industry.

The wage elasticities obtained from estimating equation (C.2) over the period 1947–1978 are much smaller than those obtained from estimating equations (C.1a) and (C.1b). Moreover, the estimate of α_2 is sensitive to the time period over which it is estimated. As suggested above, feedback from the wage variable to the demand for retail goods and services may induce a positive bias in the estimated wage elasticity. Such a bias is not likely to affect the estimate of β_1, the elasticity of substitution between retail goods and retail labor in equation (C.3). Thus, it is not surprising that the estimates of β_1 are uniformly negative and statistically significant, larger in absolute value than those of α_2, and much less sensitive to the choice of time period. The estimates of β_1 when total hours is the dependent variable are not larger than when employment is the dependent variable, except when trend is omitted. Since trend is not statistically significant by conventional standards in equation (C.3), these estimates provide some support for the hypothesis that employers' adjustment of total hours demanded in response to a change in the wage rate will be greater than the adjustment of the number of workers employed.[3]

Equation (C.3) can be used to calculate the impact of an increase in the minimum wage on the quantity of labor demanded by moving the denominator of the dependent variable to the right side and taking

[3] M. Ishaq Nadiri and Sherwin Rosen, *A Disequilibrium Model of Demand for Factors of Production*, National Bureau of Economic Research General Series no. 99 (New York: National Bureau of Economic Research, 1973), chapter 2.

TABLE C2

GLS Estimates of the Consumer's Demand for Retail Labor, Equations (C.2) and (C.3)
(asymptotic *t*-values in parentheses)[a]

Row	*Equation*	$\ln \frac{Y}{pop}$	$\ln \frac{W_r^* + \Delta W_r^*}{\Pi_r}$	$\ln \frac{\Pi_w}{\Pi_r}$	$\ln \frac{W_r^* + \Delta W_r^*}{\Pi_w}$	*T*	*Durbin-Watson*	*Rho (final iteration)*
				1947–1978				
				Dependent variable employment				
1	C.2	0.50	−0.20	0.39		0.00079	1.5	0.94
		(3.3)	(1.4)	(0.9)		(0.2)		
2		0.52	−0.13	0.38			1.5	0.95
		(3.9)	(1.5)	(0.8)				
3	C.3				−0.71	0.0027	1.7	0.64
					(4.0)	(0.6)		
4					−0.60		1.8	0.60
					(16.6)			
				Dependent variable total hours				
5	C.2	0.48	−0.14	0.60		−0.0076	1.6	0.93
		(3.3)	(1.1)	(1.4)		(1.9)		
6		0.33	−0.27	0.79			1.4	0.93
		(2.5)	(2.3)	(1.8)				
7	C.3				−0.70	−0.0050	1.8	0.73
					(4.2)	(1.2)		
8					−0.88		1.7	0.81
					(16.0)			

(Table continued on next page)

TABLE C2 (Continued)

Row	*Equation*	$\ln \frac{Y}{pop}$	$\ln \frac{W_r^* + \Delta W_r^*}{\Pi_r}$	$\ln \frac{\Pi_w}{\Pi_r}$	$\ln \frac{W_r^* + \Delta W_r^*}{\Pi_w}$	*T*	*Durbin-Watson*	*Rho (final iteration)*
				1960–1978				
				Dependent variable employment				
9	C.2	0.31	0.20	0.81		0.0018	1.4	0.68
		(1.6)	(0.9)	(1.5)		(0.3)		
10		0.36	0.23	0.82			1.4	0.70
		(2.3)	(1.2)	(1.5)				
11	C.3				−0.82	0.0039	1.5	0.69
					(3.1)	(0.7)		
12					−0.65		1.6	0.70
					(7.4)			
				Dependent variable total hours				
13	C.2	0.30	0.38	1.1		−0.010	1.6	0.63
		(1.7)	(2.0)	(2.3)		(2.0)		
14		0.70	0.70	0.99			1.5	0.50
		(0.5)	(1.1)	(1.9)				
15	C.3				−0.71	−0.0075	1.5	0.79
					(3.1)	(1.5)		
16					−1.0		1.3	0.76
					(11.6)			

[a] Degrees of freedom = number of observations.

the differential of ln e_{rt} with respect to $\ln(W_{rt}^* + \Delta W_{rt}^*)$, obtaining

$$d \ln e_{rt} = \beta_1 d \ln(W_{rt}^* + \Delta W_{rt}^*) \tag{C.4a}$$

or

$$\frac{d\, e_{rt}}{e_{rt}} = \beta_1 \frac{d(W_{rt}^* + \Delta W_{rt}^*)}{W_{rt}^* + \Delta W_{rt}^*} \tag{C.4b}$$

Thus, β_1 of equation (C.4a) and α_1' of equation (C.1b) provide approximately comparable measures of the effect of an increase in the minimum wage rate on the demand for retail labor, except that per capita sales is held constant in the latter formulation, but not in the former. Insofar as an increase in the price of retail services influences sales negatively, we should expect α_1' to exceed β_1, which is what their estimates imply.

In order to test the robustness of the estimates of the effect of minimum wage rates on the demand for retail labor, equation (C.2) has been modified as follows:

$$\ln \frac{e_{rt}}{pop_t} = \gamma_0 + \gamma_1 \ln \frac{Y_t}{pop_t} + \gamma_2 \ln \frac{W_{rt}^*}{\Pi_{rt}} + \gamma_3 \frac{\Delta W_{rt}^*}{W_{rt}^*} + \gamma_4 \ln \frac{\Pi_{wt}}{\Pi_{rt}} + \gamma_5 T \tag{C.2a}$$

In equation (C.2a), the forecast wage and the variable representing the impact of the minimum wage are entered separately. This permits analysis of the response of the quantity of labor to the average price of labor of all skills as well as to the impact of the minimum wage, which directly affects the price of labor in the lowest skill categories only. Estimates of this modified consumer's demand equation for retail labor are shown in table C3. The estimated values of γ_2 are quite similar to those of α_2 in equation (C.2), and are much less negative than the estimated values of γ_3. The estimated values of γ_3 are very close to those of α_1' in equation (C.1b), except for the employment equation estimated over the 1960–1978 period. Evidently, increases in the minimum wage do reduce the quantity of labor demanded in the retail trade industry, and the quantitative impact estimated through three different equations is quite robust.

Minimum Wage Rates and the Demand for Labor within Retail Trade

The effect of minimum wage legislation on employment is not likely to be uniform across the various subcategories of retail trade because of differences in the skill levels of workers hired and opportunities for substitution against low-wage labor. Thus, retail firms that rely on a high proportion of low-wage labor and are unable to maintain

TABLE C3

GLS Estimates of the Modified Consumer's Demand for Retail Labor, Equation (C.2a)

(asymptotic *t*-values in parentheses)[a]

$\ln \frac{Y}{pop}$	$\ln \frac{W_r^*}{\Pi_r}$	$\ln \frac{\Delta W_r^*}{W_r^*}$	$\ln \frac{\Pi_w}{\Pi_r}$	T	*Durbin-Watson*	*Rho (final iteration)*
			1947–1978			
			Dependent variable employment			
0.53	−0.22	−0.71	0.31	0.0012	1.5	0.93
(3.5)	(1.6)	(1.4)	(0.7)	(0.3)		
0.55	−0.20	−0.68	0.29		1.6	0.93
(4.1)	(1.7)	(1.4)	(0.64)			
			Dependent variable hours			
0.52	−0.18	−1.06	0.46	−0.0069	1.8	0.90
(3.8)	(1.4)	(2.3)	(1.1)	(1.9)		
0.39	−0.31	−1.29	0.63		1.6	0.89
(3.1)	(2.8)	(2.7)	(1.5)			
			1960–1978			
			Dependent variable employment			
0.39	0.11	−0.48	0.54	0.0022	1.5	0.62
(1.9)	(0.5)	(0.8)	(1.0)	(0.4)		
0.44	0.15	−0.42	0.56		1.5	0.63
(2.7)	(0.8)	(0.8)	(1.0)			
			Dependent variable hours			
0.44	0.16	−1.02	0.26	−0.0083	1.7	0.29
(3.0)	(0.9)	(2.2)	(0.6)	(1.8)		
0.32	−0.095	−1.46	−0.17		1.7	0.07
(2.6)	(0.6)	(3.0)	(0.4)			

[a] Degrees of freedom = number of observations.

a strong competitive position by substituting higher-skilled labor or capital for workers directly affected by minimum wage legislation are likely to decline in importance relative to the remainder of the industry as a result of extensions in minimum wage coverage and increases in minimum wage levels.

Examination of employment trends suggests that, within retail trade, employment in department stores may have been least affected by minimum wage legislation and, indeed, that the growth of department stores relative to the remainder of the industry has been accelerated by minimum wages. A possible reason for this acceleration is that department stores have a greater opportunity to absorb increased labor costs through consolidation of sales checkout stations, computerization of inventory controls, and the like, than do retail outlets that deal in a narrower range of merchandise, such as variety stores. One way for employers to economize on ever more expensive labor is to raise productivity by causing employees to work with more expensive merchandise. Thus, it is probably no accident that the most rapidly growing firm in the department store category once operated only variety stores.

Casual observation also suggests that food stores, because of the nature of the merchandise sold, have been able to take advantage of much mechanization and automation in response to rising labor costs, and that considerable substitution against labor is likely to be observed as wage rates rise. Although gasoline service stations have been traditional employers of low-wage labor and would be an important subject of study, we are unfortunately precluded from analyzing employment over time in this category of retail trade by lack of data.

Minimum Wage Rates and Employment in Department and Variety Stores. Between 1958 (the first year for which data are available) and 1978, nonsupervisory employment in department stores relative to all retail trade excluding eating and drinking places grew from 13.7 percent to 18.6 percent. Statistical analysis suggests that an important component of employment shifts within the department store industry and between department stores and the rest of retail trade can be attributed to minimum wage legislation. The approach adopted to study these trends is quite similar to that used in the analysis of retail employment in the preceding section. The following variables have been adapted or differ from the study of all retail trade. The data sources are the same, except where specified to the contrary.

$D \equiv$ dummy variable equal to 0 for 1958–1967 and equal to 1 for 1968–1978. Sales data after 1967 are not comparable to those before 1968. Source: U.S. Bureau of the Census, *Historical Statistics of the United States, Colonial Times to 1970* (1975).

$W_{dt}, W_{vt} \equiv$ mean average hourly earnings of nonsupervisory workers in department stores and variety stores, respectively. These variables are available only after 1957.

$\Pi_{dt}, \Pi_{vt} \equiv$ the GNP deflator for department store and variety store sales, respectively. Source: unpublished data of the U.S. Department of Commerce, Bureau of Economic Analysis. These variables are not available for years before 1959.

$\Pi_{wdt}, \Pi_{wvt} \equiv$ index of retailers' cost of goods, calculated by multiplying Π_{wt} by the ratio Π_{dt}/Π_{rt} or Π_{vt}/Π_{rt}, respectively.

$S_{dt}, S_{vt} \equiv$ total sales of department stores and variety stores, respectively.

$e_{dt}, e_{vt} \equiv$ employment or total hours of work of nonsupervisory employees in department stores and variety stores, respectively.

$M_{gt} \equiv$ the minimum wage rate applicable to department stores and variety stores. Since the proportion of workers covered by federal minimum wage legislation in 1961 was nearly 100 percent in department stores and nearly 70 percent in variety stores, only the basic minimum for retail trade was used to calculate M_{gt}.[4]

$\Delta W_{dt}^*/W_{dt}^*$,
$\Delta W_{vt}^*/W_{vt}^* \equiv$ proportionate increase in the forecast wage required to bring all workers to at least the minimum wage. $W_{dt}^* \equiv 0.95\, W_{rt}^*$ and $W_{vt}^* \equiv 0.67\, W_{rt}^*$. These ratios are based on the values of W_{dt} and W_{vt} for the years 1958–1961. The mean values of W_{dt} and W_{vt} relative to W_{rt} over this period are 0.95 and 0.67, with standard deviations of 0.004 and 0.007, respectively. The Δ's are computed similarly to those for all retail trade, based on 1956 wage distribution estimates:

$$f\left(\frac{W_d}{\overline{W}_d}\right) = \underset{(4.6)}{-0.055} + \underset{(7.1)}{0.152}\left(\frac{W_d}{\overline{W}_d}\right)$$

$$0.300 \leq \frac{W_d}{\overline{W}_d} \leq 0.725 \qquad \overline{R}^2 = .83$$

and

$$f\left(\frac{W_v}{\overline{W}_v}\right) = \underset{(2.0)}{-0.149} + \underset{(2.8)}{0.528}\left(\frac{W_v}{\overline{W}_v}\right) - 0.300\left(\frac{W_v}{\overline{W}_v}\right)^2$$

$$0.449 \leq \frac{W_v}{\overline{W}_v} \leq 1.12 \qquad \overline{R}^2 = .47$$

(t-values in parentheses)

[4] U.S. Department of Labor, Wage and Hours and Public Contracts Divisions, *Retail Trade: An Interim Study of the Effects of the 1961 Amendments* (1966), and *Retail Trade: A Study of the Effects of the 1961 Amendments* (1967).

TABLE C4

GLS Estimates of Equation (C.1b) and Modifications for Department Stores and Variety Stores

(absolute values of asymptotic *t*-ratios in parentheses)[a]

	U_m	T	Durbin-Watson	Rho (final iteration)
$\frac{\Delta W_d^*}{W_d^*}$	*Dependent Variable e_d 1960–1978 (Employment)*			
0.28	−2.65	0.028	0.9	0.89
(0.8)	(5.9)	(11.9)		
	Dependent Variable e_d 1960–1978 (Total Hours)			
0.082	−2.79	0.018	0.9	0.92
(0.2)	(5.9)	(6.6)		
	Dependent Variable e_d/e_r 1959–1978 (Employment)			
0.82	−1.15	0.014	1.3	0.93
(2.3)	(3.2)	(6.8)		
	Dependent Variable e_d/e_r 1959–1978 (Total Hours)			
1.04	−1.32	0.013	1.1	0.93
(2.4)	(3.0)	(5.0)		
$\frac{\Delta W_v^*}{W_v^*}$	*Dependent Variable $e_v/(e_v+e_d)$ 1958–1978 (Employment)*			
−0.24	−0.41	−0.033	1.4	0.82
(2.4)	(0.9)	(16.5)		
	Dependent Variable $e_v/(e_v+e_d)$ 1958–1978 (Total Hours)			
−0.18	0.52	−0.031	1.6	0.79
(1.6)	(1.0)	(14.6)		

[a] Degrees of freedom = number of observations.

The results of estimating equation (C.1b) for department stores are shown in table C4. (The estimates of equations C.1b, C.2, C.2a, and C.3 are not sensitive to whether they are based on the period 1958–1978, 1959–1978, or 1960–1978.) In contrast to the results for all retail trade, the minimum wage variable is uncorrelated with either per capita department store employment or with per capita total hours. The remainder of table C4 shows the results of estimating two modified versions of equation (C.1b). In the first modification, the dependent variable is the ratio of department store employment or total hours to the comparable variable for all retail trade. In the second modification, the dependent variable is the ratio of variety store employment or total hours to the sum of these variables for department and variety stores (essentially the retail category, general merchandise); the minimum wage variable is changed from $\Delta W_d^*/W_d^*$ to $\Delta W_v^*/W_v^*$. The results of estimating these modified equations do imply, as discussed above, that the retail trade minimum wage has accelerated the relative expansion of the department store industry. An increase in the minimum wage that would raise the average department store forecast wage by 1 percent is associated with an increase of about 0.8 percent in the share of department store employment in all retail employment and with an increase of about 1 percent in its share in all retail total hours. A 1 percent increase in the forecast wage of variety stores resulting from the retail minimum wage is associated with a decline in the share of variety store employment in total general merchandise employment of approximately one-quarter percent and with a decline in its share in total hours of slightly less than 0.2 percent. (Variety store employees made up an average of about 20 percent of the sum of variety and department store employees over the 1958–1978 period.)

The results of estimating the demand equations (C.2), (C.2a), and (C.3) are contained in table C5. The estimates of equation (C.2), which represents the consumer's demand for department store labor, are consistent with the basic hypothesis that an increase in the price of labor reduces the quantity demanded, despite the fact that for department stores the equation must be estimated over the 1959–1978 period. The estimated elasticity of demand with respect to the wage variable is at least three times larger than for all retail trade estimated over the 1947–1978 period. Recall that, when equation (C.2) is estimated for all retail trade over the 1960–1978 period, there is no evidence that an increase in the average wage reduces the quantity of labor demanded, although the opposite is true when the estimate is based on the 1947–1978 period. The coefficient of real per capita disposable personal income is much higher for department stores than for all retail trade.

In estimates of the modified consumer demand equation (C.2a), the coefficient of the minimum wage variable remains insignificantly different from zero when per capita employment is the dependent variable, but the *t*-value and magnitude of the coefficient are much more negative when the dependent variable is total hours per capita, compared with the coefficient of the minimum wage variable in equation (C.1b). The smaller (in absolute value) magnitude of the coefficient of the minimum wage variable in equation (C.2a) for department stores than for all retail trade—even with per capita income, the forecast wage, and the price of goods held constant—reinforces the belief that minimum wage legislation has accelerated the growth of the department stores relative to all retail trade.

Estimation of equation (C.3) for department stores—and for every other subcategory of retail trade—is hampered by a break in the comparability of sales data between 1967 and 1968. In an attempt to control for this discontinuity in the data, a dummy variable has been added to equation (C.3) when it is applied to department stores and other retail industry divisions. This is an admittedly crude procedure, and it may account for an anomaly in the estimates of equation (C.3). The results in table C5 correspond closely to those for all retail trade in table C2 when trend is excluded from the equation. Since the coefficient of the trend variable in equation (C.3) is highly insignificant when the ratio of employment to sales is the dependent variable, omission of the trend variable, and avoiding the problem of collinearity with the wage variable, is not troublesome. The coefficient of trend is highly significant, however, when the ratio of total hours to sales is the dependent variable, and the coefficient of the wage variable, when it is included, is positive and statistically significant. When trend is excluded from the equation, the coefficient of the wage variable reverses sign and retains about the same asymptotic *t*-value, and its magnitude is approximately equal to that for all retail trade and is somewhat larger in absolute value than when the dependent variable is the ratio of employment to sales.

Minimum Wage Rates and Employment in Food Stores. The equations and independent variables used to analyze the impact of minimum wage legislation on employment and total hours in food stores, and the sources of data, are the same as those used for all retail trade and for department stores, with the following exceptions:

$W_{ft} \equiv$ mean average hourly earnings of nonsupervisory workers in food stores. This variable is available only after 1957.

$\Pi_{ft} \equiv$ the GNP deflator for food store sales.

$\Pi_{wft} \equiv$ index of food retailers' cost of goods: $\Pi_{wft} = \Pi_{wt} \cdot \Pi_{ft} / \Pi_{rt}$.

$S_{ft} \equiv$ total food store sales.

$e_{ft} \equiv$ employment or total hours of work of nonsupervisory employees in food stores.

TABLE C5

GLS ESTIMATES OF EQUATIONS (C.2), (C.2a), AND (C.3) FOR DEPARTMENT STORES, 1959–1978
(absolute values of asymptotic t-ratios in parentheses)[a]

Equation	*D*	$\ln \frac{Y}{pop}$	$\ln \frac{W_d^* + \Delta W_d^*}{\Pi_d}$	$\ln \frac{\Pi_{wd}}{\Pi_d}$	$\ln \frac{W_d^* + \Delta W_d^*}{\Pi_{wd}}$	$\ln \frac{W_d^*}{\Pi_d}$	$\frac{\Delta W_d^*}{W_d^*}$	*T*	*Durbin-Watson*	*Rho (final iteration)*
				Dependent Variable Employment						
C.2		1.25	−0.63	0.057				0.014	1.7	0.28
		(6.5)	(2.6)	(0.08)				(1.6)		
C.2a		1.14		0.68		−0.56	−0.064	0.015	1.5	0.51
		(5.5)		(1.0)		(2.3)	(0.1)	(1.8)		
C.3	−0.34				−0.44			−0.012	1.1	0.94
	(5.0)				(0.4)			(0.4)		
	−0.34				−0.81				1.0	0.95
	(5.2)				(1.9)					

Equation	D	$\ln \frac{Y}{pop}$	$\ln \frac{W_d^* + \Delta W_d^*}{\Pi_d}$	$\ln \frac{\Pi_{wd}}{\Pi_d}$	$\ln \frac{W_d^* + \Delta W_d^*}{\Pi_{wd}}$	$\ln \frac{W_d^*}{\Pi_d}$	$\frac{\Delta W_d^*}{W_d^*}$	T	*Durbin-Watson*	*Rho (final iteration)*
				Dependent Variable Total Hours						
C.2		1.41	−0.72	0.48				0.0026	1.8	0.24
		(8.6)	(3.5)	(0.8)				(0.3)		
		1.45	−0.66	0.41					1.8	0.24
		(13.8)	(6.2)	(0.8)						
C.2a		1.37		0.70		−0.69	−0.51	0.0027	1.8	0.37
		(7.7)		(1.1)		(3.2)	(1.2)	(0.4)		
		1.42		0.61		−0.63	−0.46		1.8	0.36
		(11.3)		(1.0)		(5.0)	(1.2)			
C.3	−0.31				1.69			−0.080	1.4	0.55
	(8.5)				(3.4)			(6.0)		
	−0.33				−0.92				1.2	0.90
	(6.4)				(3.1)					

[a] Degrees of freedom = number of observations.

$M_{ft} \equiv$ see M_{gt} above.

$\frac{\Delta W_{ft}^*}{W_{ft}^*} \equiv$ proportionate increase in the forecast wage required to bring all workers to at least the minimum wage. The standard deviation of $W_{ft} \div W_{rt}$ over this period is 0.011. The calculation of ΔW_{ft}^* is based on the 1956 wage distribution estimate:

$$f\left(\frac{W_f}{\overline{W}_f}\right) = \underset{(1.3)}{-0.017} + \underset{(3.6)}{0.089} \frac{W_f}{\overline{W}_f}$$

$$0.276 \leq \frac{W_f}{\overline{W}_f} \leq 0.690 \qquad \overline{R}^2 = .55$$

(t-values in parentheses)

Estimates of equations (C.1b), (C.2), and (C.3) for food stores are contained in table C6. The results for equation (C.1b) imply that minimum wage rates have reduced employment in food stores, with the impact being somewhat smaller than for all retail trade. When total hours are the measure of the quantity of labor demanded, the impact of minimum wages is larger in absolute value, but only a little more than half as large as for all retail trade. The consumer demand equation (C.2) indicates a negative and statistically significant response of the quantity of labor demanded to the wage rate only when employment is the dependent variable. The results for equation (C.3), however, imply a pronounced tendency to substitute away from labor in response to an increase in its price, just as for all retail trade.

Minimum Wage Rates in Retail Trade and Employment of Young Persons

In order to estimate the impact of minimum wage legislation on teenage employment and unemployment, regression equations were estimated over two time periods, 1947–1978 and 1960–1978. The following variables were included in the regressions:

dependent variables

$E_{it} \equiv$ the fraction of all persons in the ith age group employed in year t (including military personnel).

$U_{it} \equiv$ the fraction of all persons in the ith age group unemployed in year t.
Source: U.S. Bureau of the Census, March Current Population Surveys; these and all other data from the March

Current Population Surveys were assembled by J. Peter Mattila, who kindly supplied them to me.

independent variables

$P_t \equiv$ population age 15–24 ÷ population age 15–64.

$M_t \equiv$ the number of military personnel ÷ population 15–64.

$U_{mt} \equiv$ the unemployment rate of men ages 35–54 in year t.

$E_{it} \equiv$ a variable reflecting the impact of minimum wage legislation on the average cost of labor outside retail trade.

$\frac{\Delta W_{rt}^*}{W_{rt}^*} \equiv$ a variable reflecting the impact of minimum wage legislation on the cost of labor in retail trade.

$T_t \equiv$ a trend variable equal to 1 for the first year of data.

The rationale for inclusion of these variables is straightforward and has been developed in other studies.[5] The major distinction between the approach taken here and elsewhere is the inclusion of two variables representing the impact of minimum wages—one for retail trade and another for the rest of the economy—since this focuses on the impact of retail trade minimum wage legislation. The major question of interest is whether minimum wage rates in retail trade reduce employment and affect unemployment of young persons, in addition to the impact of minimum wages imposed on the rest of the economy. Because minimum wages increase earnings prospects in covered employment, reduce wages in noncovered jobs, and reduce the number of jobs in covered establishments, other things being equal, the relationship between minimum wages and unemployment is uncertain.[6]

The remaining variables, along with the two minimum wage variables, are incorporated in a reduced form employment equation. The proportion of persons aged fifteen to twenty-four in the population (P) will be negatively correlated with the employment rate of young

[5] See, for example, Nabeel Al-Salam, Aline Quester, and Finis Welch, "Some Determinants of the Level and Racial Composition of Teenage Employment," in Simon Rottenberg, ed., *The Economics of Legal Minimum Wages* (Washington, D.C.: American Enterprise Institute, forthcoming); Jacob Mincer, "Unemployment Effects of Minimum Wages," *Journal of Political Economy*, vol. 84, no. 4, part 2 (August 1976), pp. S87-S104; and Finis Welch, "Minimum Wage Legislation in the United States," in Orley Ashenfelter and James Blum, eds., *Evaluating the Labor Market Effects of Social Programs* (Princeton, N.J.: Princeton University Industrial Relations Section, 1977), pp. 14-23.

[6] Mincer, "Unemployment Effects of Minimum Wages."

TABLE C6

GLS ESTIMATES OF EQUATIONS (C.1b), (C.2), AND (C.3) FOR FOOD STORES

(absolute values of asymptotic *t*-ratios in parentheses)[a]

Row	Equation	D	$\frac{\Delta W_f^*}{W_f}$	U_m	$\ln\frac{Y}{pop}$	$\ln\frac{W_f^*+\Delta W_f^*}{\Pi_f}$	$\ln\frac{\Pi_{wf}}{\Pi_f}$	$\ln\frac{W_f^*+\Delta W_f^*}{\Pi_{wf}}$	T	Durbin-Watson	Rho (final iteration)
					1960–1978						
					Dependent variable employment						
1	C.1b		−0.62 (1.7)	−0.010 (0.02)					0.017 (12.8)	1.1	0.62
					Dependent variable total hours						
2			−0.81 (2.1)	−0.36 (0.8)					0.0094 (3.3)	1.0	0.93
					1959–1978						
					Dependent variable employment						
3	C.2				−0.18 (1.0)	−0.23 (1.9)	0.069 (0.1)		0.023 (4.7)	0.90	0.86

4			0.47 (3.4)	−0.11 (0.7)	−0.015 (0.0)			1.4	0.97
5	C.3	−0.079 (4.1)				−0.69 (5.4)	0.0062 (2.9)	1.7	0.61
			Dependent variable total hours						
6	C.2		−0.16 (0.8)	−0.10 (0.8)	0.86 (1.4)		0.014 (2.5)	0.76	0.95
7			0.22 (1.7)	−0.028 (0.2)	0.90 (1.3)			0.90	0.98
8	C.3	−0.092 (4.6)				−0.64 (4.8)	−0.00099 (0.3)	1.6	0.91
9		−0.094 (4.9)				−0.65 (5.5)		1.6	0.89

[a] Degrees of freedom = number of observations.

persons insofar as they are not perfect substitutes for older workers. The variable representing the proportion of military personnel in the population is included to reflect the impact of the reduction in the size of the young male civilian population during periods of war and increased employment opportunities for those young persons who remain in the civilian population. There is an element of endogeneity in this variable, since one effect of minimum wage legislation—through a reduction in civilian employment opportunities—may be to increase military enlistments. This variable is expected to be positively correlated with the employment rate of all groups. The unemployment rate of adult males reflects aggregate labor market conditions and should be negatively related to employment rates.

The estimated employment and unemployment equations are presented in table C7. For the 1947–1978 period, two versions of the employment equations are shown in most cases, the second version omitting variables whose coefficients are smaller than their asymptotic *t*-ratios. Only the second version of the employment equation is presented for the 1960–1978 period and for the unemployment equation estimated over both 1947–1978 and 1960–1978.

Minimum wage rates in retail trade have had a pronounced negative impact on the employment of males aged eighteen and nineteen. It is particularly striking that the retail trade minimum wage variable dominates the variable representing minimum wage rates elsewhere. An increase in the retail trade minimum wage that raises the forecast mean wage by 1 percent is associated with a decline in the employment rate of eighteen- and nineteen-year-olds of 1.1 percent, based on the 1960–1978 estimate. The estimated impact of retail trade minimum wage rates is negative and marginally significant over the 1947–1978 period, but neither minimum wage variable is significantly related to the employment of fourteen- to seventeen-year-olds over the 1960–1978 period. The two minimum wage variables are significantly related to the employment rate of males aged twenty to twenty-four only over the 1960–1978 period, and they are opposite in sign. The positive coefficient of the retail trade variable suggests that an increase in the retail trade minimum wage induces a substitution of twenty- to twenty-four-year-old males for eighteen- and nineteen-year-old males—a not surprising result. The combined impact of minimum wage increases that raise the mean wage in retail trade and elsewhere by 1 percent is a decline in the employment rate of twenty- to twenty-four-year-olds of 1.29 percentage points.

Retail trade minimum wage rates appear to have had a pronounced negative impact on the employment rate of females aged fourteen to seventeen. The evidence is more pronounced when the

TABLE C7

GLS ESTIMATES OF EMPLOYMENT AND UNEMPLOYMENT EQUATIONS

(asymptotic t-ratios in parentheses)[a]

Row	Age/Sex	$\frac{\Delta W_r^*}{W_r^*}$	$0.01E_1$	U_m	P	M	T	Durbin-Watson	Rho (final iteration)
				Dependent Variable Employment/Population					
				1947–1978					
1	14–17/Males	−0.90	0.80	−1.39	−0.050	−2.30	−0.0020	2.0	0.49
		(1.2)	(0.7)	(3.8)	(0.1)	(2.5)	(1.8)		
2		−0.70		−1.42		−2.10	−0.0022	2.0	0.43
		(1.8)		(4.1)		(3.0)	(3.2)		
				1960–1978					
3		0.017		−1.57	−0.58	−2.97	0.0012	1.8	−0.44
		(0.04)		(6.1)	(2.1)	(1.9)	(1.0)		
				1947–1978					
4	18–19/Males	−1.53	−0.29	−2.41	−0.36	−0.51	−0.0019	1.9	0.64
		(1.6)	(0.2)	(5.3)	(0.5)	(0.4)	(0.1)		
5		−1.85		−2.32			−0.0024	1.9	0.63
		(3.2)		(5.6)			(2.3)		
				1960–1978					
6		−1.12		−2.14	−1.24		0.0052	1.6	0.27
		(2.6)		(4.7)	(2.1)		(2.4)		

(Table continued on next page)

TABLE C7 (Continued)

Row	Age/Sex	$\frac{\Delta W_r^*}{W_r^*}$	$0.01E_1$	U_m	P	M	T	Durbin-Watson	Rho (final iteration)
				1947–1978					
7	20–24/Males	0.082	−0.053	−2.01	−1.53	0.10	0.0021	1.8	0.16
		(0.14)	(0.06)	(6.0)	(4.1)	(0.14)	(3.0)		
8		−0.085		−2.03	−1.55		0.0022	1.8	0.17
		(0.3)		(7.1)	(7.1)		(3.3)		
				1960–1978					
9		0.31	−1.6	−2.41	−1.22			2.3	−0.35
		(1.8)	(5.0)	(18.9)	(21.2)				
				1947–1978					
10	14–17/Females	−0.46	0.41	−0.97	−0.42	−1.98	0.0030	1.7	0.84
		(1.0)	(0.6)	(4.6)	(0.9)	(3.4)	(2.6)		
11		−0.45		−0.97		−1.85	0.0020	1.6	0.80
		(1.4)		(4.5)		(3.4)	(2.6)		
				1960–1978					
12		−0.56		−1.15	−0.85		0.0080	1.7	0.35
		(2.4)		(4.8)	(2.6)		(6.8)		
				1947–1978					
13	18–19/Females	−0.30	−1.89	−1.15	−0.25	−1.04	0.00056	1.9	0.45
		(0.4)	(1.4)	(2.6)	(0.4)	(0.9)	(0.4)		
14		−0.34	−1.98	−0.95				1.9	0.49
		(0.7)	(1.7)	(2.4)					

				1960–1978					
15		−0.31		−1.31	−1.77		0.010	2.2	−0.22
		(1.1)		(3.9)	(4.8)		(7.5)		
				1947–1978					
16	20–24/Females	0.011	0.88	−0.80	0.024	−1.73	0.0057	2.2	0.89
		(0.02)	(0.9)	(2.6)	(0.04)	(2.0)	(3.1)		
17		0.32		−0.85		−1.86	0.0054	2.2	0.86
		(0.7)		(2.8)		(2.3)	(4.0)		
				1960–1978					
18		−0.051		−1.66	−1.20		0.015	1.9	0.39
		(0.2)		(6.0)	(3.1)		(10.6)		
				Dependent Variable Unemployment/Population					
				1947–1978					
19	14–17/Males	−0.29		0.30	0.26		0.00082	2.0	0.15
		(2.9)		(3.0)	(3.4)		(3.6)		
				1960–1968					
20		−0.43		0.23		1.48	0.0032	2.2	−0.37
		(2.4)		(2.1)		(2.1)	(6.1)		
				1947–1978					
21	18–19/Males	0.090		1.12		−0.93	0.0014	2.0	0.05
		(0.6)		(6.0)		(3.3)	(5.3)		
				1960–1978					
22		−0.58	0.10	1.49	0.31		0.0012	2.1	−0.04
		(2.5)	(2.2)	(8.3)	(1.6)		(1.6)		

(Table continued on next page)

TABLE C7 (Continued)

Row	Age/Sex	$\frac{\Delta W_r^*}{W_r^*}$	$0.01E_1$	U_m	P	M	T	Durbin-Watson	Rho (final iteration)
				1947–1978					
23	20–24/Males	−0.64	0.69	1.59	0.59			2.1	−0.28
		(2.5)	(1.5)	(11.2)	(6.6)				
				1960–1978					
24		−0.92	1.56	2.08	0.72	0.76	0.00062	2.2	−0.72
		(4.5)	(5.8)	(18.7)	(5.9)	(1.0)	(1.2)		
				1947–1978					
25	14–17/Females	−0.33		0.21	0.28		0.00088	1.7	0.44
		(4.0)		(3.1)	(4.1)		(4.4)		
				1960–1978					
26		−0.57	0.56	0.34	0.15	0.73	0.0025	2.0	−0.005
		(3.2)	(1.19)	(3.0)	(1.2)	(1.1)	(4.4)		
				1947–1978					
27	18–19/Females	0.33	−0.55	0.75	0.16		0.0015	2.0	−0.13
		(1.7)	(1.6)	(6.5)	(1.8)		(6.7)		
				1960–1978					
28		0.033		0.62			0.0022	2.4	−0.44
		(0.3)		(4.8)			(15.4)		

				1947–1978					
29	20–24/Females	0.022	−0.30	0.72	0.22		0.001	1.9	0.14
		(0.1)	(1.1)	(7.8)	(2.7)		(5.0)		
				1960–1978					
30		−0.17		1.08	0.19	1.13	0.0022	1.9	−0.02
		(0.8)		(7.3)	(1.2)	(1.4)	(3.0)		

[a] Degrees of freedom = number of observations.

estimate is based on the 1960–1978 estimate, which begins the year before the extension of minimum wage legislation to the retail trade industry. The magnitude of the impact is about one-half as great as that for males aged eighteen and nineteen. The estimated impact of retail trade minimum wage rates is not significant for either eighteen- and nineteen-year-old females or for those in the twenty- to twenty-four-year age group.

The unemployment-population ratio is negatively and significantly related to retail trade minimum wage rates for males of all three age groups. The only exception is the longer, 1947–1978 period for eighteen- and nineteen-year-olds, which encompasses fourteen years before the extension of retail trade legislation to the retail trade industry. Minimum wage rates in other industries, however, apparently increased unemployment among twenty- to twenty-four-year-old males, offsetting the negative impact of the retail trade minimum. Adding up the employment and unemployment impacts of minimum wages yields the effect on labor force participation, which is negative for teenagers and negligible for males aged twenty to twenty-four. Among females, the impact of retail trade minimum wage rates on the unemployment of fourteen- to seventeen-year-olds is negative and statistically significant. When the equation is estimated over the 1960–1978 period, however, the estimated impact of minimum wages in other industries is positive and about equal in magnitude. For the other two groups of females, minimum wage rates in retail trade appear to have had a negligible impact on the employment-population ratio. For eighteen- and nineteen-year-olds, the 1947–1978 estimate is positive and marginally significant, but it is offset by the estimated impact of minimum wage rates in other industries.

Appendix D

Minimum Wage Regulation in Retail Trade and Investments in Human Capital

School Attendance

In order to estimate the influence of minimum wage regulation in retail trade on school attendance, regression equations were estimated with annual data over two time periods, 1947–1978 and 1960–1978. The following dependent variable was included in the regressions:

> $S_{it} \equiv$ the proportion of all persons in the ith age group enrolled in school in year t, separated for males and females; i = 14–17, 18–19, 20–24; t = 1947, . . . , 1978. Source: U.S. Bureau of the Census, March Current Population Surveys.

The independent variables are the same as those used in the analysis of the employment and unemployment of young persons. The rationale for including these variables in a reduced-form schooling equation is similar to that for including them in the wage equations and employment equations developed in Appendixes B and C.[1] Variables influencing wages and employment are also expected to affect schooling decisions. Their expected influence on schooling is ambiguous because, as pointed out in chapter 4, an improvement in labor market opportunities may either increase or decrease school attendance.

The results of estimating regression equations with these variables are shown in table D1. For each age-sex group and for both time periods, regressions with all six independent variables are shown, as well as regressions from which some of the variables that are insignificant by commonly accepted standards have been omitted.

---

[1] See also Nabeel Al-Salam, Aline Quester, and Finis Welch, "Some Determinants of the Level and Racial Composition of Teenage Employment," in Simon Rottenberg, ed., *The Economics of Legal Minimum Wages* (Washington, D.C.: American Enterprise Institute, forthcoming).

TABLE D1

GLS ESTIMATES OF SCHOOLING EQUATIONS, DEPENDENT VARIABLE PROPORTION OF ALL PERSONS ENROLLED IN SCHOOL (OCTOBER)

(asymptotic *t*-ratios in parentheses)[a]

Age/Sex	$\frac{\Delta W_r^*}{W_r^*}$	$0.01E_1$	U_m	*P*	*M*	*T*	*Durbin-Watson*	*Rho (final iteration)*
				1947–1978				
14–17/Males	0.26	0.53	0.23	−0.54	−0.035	0.0058	2.3	0.90
	(0.7)	(0.9)	(1.3)	(1.3)	(0.1)	(5.1)		
	0.091	0.64	0.23			0.0050	2.2	0.95
	(0.3)	(1.1)	(1.4)			(4.2)		
18–19/Males	3.28	2.1	0.64	−1.24	−1.40	0.0066	1.9	0.27
	(3.1)	(1.3)	(1.1)	(1.8)	(1.1)	(4.8)		
	1.92	3.3	1.02			0.0047	2.0	0.36
	(2.4)	(2.2)	(2.0)			(4.6)		
20–24/Males	0.18	0.14	0.13	1.21	−0.48	0.0004	2.0	0.80
	(0.4)	(0.02)	(0.06)	(2.7)	(0.08)	(0.03)		
	0.13			1.37			1.9	0.81
	(0.4)			(4.7)				

				1960–1978				
14–17/Males	−0.086	0.16	0.48	0.66	2.52	0.0007	1.5	0.69
	(0.4)	(0.4)	(3.8)	(3.2)	(3.6)	(0.8)		
	−0.0073		0.46	0.76	2.23		1.6	0.68
	(0.05)		(3.6)	(6.0)	(4.1)			
18–19/Males	2.45	0.27	0.20	0.77	−0.95	−0.0030	1.9	−0.013
	(2.2)	(0.2)	(0.3)	(1.0)	(0.2)	(0.9)		
	2.57			0.11			1.9	−0.005
	(6.8)			(0.5)				
20–24/Males	0.98	−1.45	0.17	1.29	0.90	−0.0018	2.2	−0.46
	(2.9)	(3.1)	(0.9)	(6.2)	(0.7)	(2.0)		
	1.15	−1.39		1.17		−0.0019	2.3	−0.51
	(5.2)	(3.2)		(6.8)		(2.8)		
				1947–1978				
14–17/Females	0.12	0.74	−0.12	−0.28	0.82	0.0049	2.2	0.75
	(0.4)	(1.4)	(0.8)	(1.0)	(2.0)	(7.1)		
	−0.061	0.95			1.07	0.0045	2.3	0.75
	(0.2)	(2.0)			(3.0)	(8.8)		
18–19/Females	0.73	1.47	0.64	0.41	0.62	0.0067	2.1	−0.23
	(1.5)	(1.9)	(1.8)	(1.3)	(1.0)	(11.2)		
	1.17	1.0	0.39			0.0072	2.1	−0.18
	(3.5)	(1.5)	(1.5)			(18.6)		

(Table continued on next page)

TABLE D1 (Continued)

Age/Sex	$\frac{\Delta W_r^*}{W_r^*}$	$0.01E_1$	U_m	P	M	T	*Durbin-Watson*	*Rho (final iteration)*
20–24/Females	−0.35	0.31	−0.065	0.58	0.20	0.0044	1.9	0.51
	(1.0)	(0.6)	(0.4)	(2.5)	(0.5)	(8.5)		
	−0.13			0.48		0.0044	1.9	0.50
	(0.6)			(2.8)		(8.9)		
				1960–1978				
14–17/Females	0.86	−0.31	−0.093	0.16	−1.11	−0.0002	1.9	−0.07
	(3.8)	(0.9)	(0.7)	(1.1)	(1.4)	(0.4)		
	0.58					0.0013	1.90	0.14
	(7.0)					(6.8)		
18–19/Females	1.31	−0.97	1.11	1.05	3.09	0.0054	1.8	−0.40
	(2.4)	(1.2)	(3.5)	(3.1)	(1.5)	(3.7)		
20–24/Females	0.075	−0.54	0.41	0.19	2.80	0.0079	2.0	−0.32
	(0.2)	(1.1)	(2.2)	(0.9)	(2.3)	(8.8)		
	0.27	−0.48	0.34		2.23	0.0082	2.0	−0.42
	(0.9)	(1.0)	(2.0)		(2.0)	(10.5)		
	0.58		0.26			0.0069	2.1	−0.44
	(4.4)		(1.5)			(36.3)		

[a] Degrees of freedom = number of observations.

Recall that Mattila has estimated a net positive impact of minimum wages on the schooling of teenagers, whereas the focus here is on the impact of retail trade minimum wages on the schooling decisions of two teenage groups, as well as on the twenty- to twenty-four-year-old age group.[2] The question that the regression equations reported in table D1 help answer is: Given the impact of minimum wage rates on the rest of the economy, what is the effect on schooling decisions of a change in the impact of minimum wage rates in retail trade alone? If we concentrate on the 1960–1978 time period, which begins in the year before the imposition of federal minimum wage regulation in retail trade, the answer to the question appears to be that minimum wage rates in retail trade have increased school attendance by eighteen- and nineteen-year-old males, fourteen- to seventeen-year-old females, and eighteen- and nineteen-year-old females. In the case of eighteen- and nineteen-year-old males and fourteen- to seventeen-year-old females, retail trade minimum wages most clearly dominate the impact of minimum wage rates in other industries. Recall that retail trade minimum wage rates have had the most pronounced disemployment effects on these two age groups. Instead of the decline in employment leading to a rise in unemployment (see table C7), it has resulted in increased school attendance. There is no net impact on the schooling decisions of fourteen- to seventeen-year-old males or twenty- to twenty-four-year-old males, and the estimated impact on twenty- to twenty-four-year-old females is highly sensitive to which variables are included in the regression. For the longer 1947–1978 period, the results for males are similar to those based on the 1960–1978 period: only the schooling decisions of eighteen- and nineteen-year-olds are affected by retail trade minimum wages. Among females, fourteen- to seventeen-year-olds are evidently influenced in their schooling decisions by minimum wage legislation, but not particularly by minimum wage rates in retail trade; eighteen- and nineteen-year-olds, however, are apparently influenced by wage floors in retail trade as well as those in other industries.

Evidently, minimum wage legislation in retail trade has had a particularly strong impact on eighteen- and nineteen-year-olds of both sexes. Using results from the 1960–1978 time period, an increase in $\Delta W_{rt}^*/W_{rt}^*$ of one standard deviation (only .23 of the maximum attained by this variable during the period) would increase the proportion of eighteen- and nineteen-year-old males enrolled in school by 0.033 and of eighteen- and nineteen-year-old females by 0.017. Al-

[2] J. Peter Mattila, "The Impact of Minimum Wages on Teenage Schooling and on the Part-Time/Full-Time Employment of Youths," in Rottenberg, ed., *The Economics of Legal Minimum Wages.*

though differences in model specification make it difficult to compare these results with those of Mattila, it is worth noting that for eighteen- and nineteen-year-olds he finds that a 10 percent increase in his minimum wage index increases the proportion of males enrolled in school by 0.0133, and the proportion of females by 0.0126.[3]

Wage Growth

With a procedure used by Edward Lazear, it is possible to use the National Longitudinal Survey (NLS) of Young Men to estimate the impact of minimum wage regulation in retail trade and other industries on wage growth and to infer from this relationship an approximation of the full wage rate.[4] That rate is defined to be the sum of the hourly rate of pay plus the present value of increased future earning power attributable to current work experience.

The analysis is confined to young men aged fourteen to nineteen because teenagers, with relatively little work experience, are most likely to accept jobs with low observed rates of pay in exchange for enhanced future earning opportunities, and because men are less likely to have their work experience interrupted by marriage and child-rearing than women. Wage growth is observed over two time periods, 1966–1969 and 1966–1971 (1966 being the first survey year in which the young men range from fourteen to nineteen years of age).

Since it is early work experience that is most likely to be performed for a subminimum rate of pay, only minimum wage coverage on the first job for which survey data are available is considered as an influence on future earning potential. That job is the current or last job held as of the first NLS survey, conducted in October 1966. Experimentation with alternative specifications of the variables measuring whether the job was affected by minimum wage legislation indicated that there is no distinct effect of early employment in retail trade on future wage growth, regardless of whether the job was covered by minimum wage legislation, as opposed to a job in any industry subject to minimum wage regulation. Therefore, the empirical work has been conducted using a variable reflecting the probability of being employed in a job covered by federal minimum wage legislation. The variable is derived from unpublished data of the

[3] Ibid.

[4] National Longitudinal Survey of Young Men, Center for Human Resource Research, Ohio State University, Columbus, Ohio. See Edward Lazear, "Age, Experience, and Wage Growth," *American Economic Review*, vol. 66, no. 4 (September 1966), pp. 548-58; and "The Narrowing of Black-White Wage Differentials Is Illusory," *American Economic Review*, vol. 69, no. 4 (September 1969), pp. 553-64.

Employment Standards Administration of the U.S. Department of Labor and measures the proportion of workers in establishments covered by federal minimum wage legislation in the major industry division of the current or last job held as of the 1966 National Longitudinal Survey.

The sample is not limited to those whose reported rate of pay on the current or last job is equal to or slightly greater than the legal minimum wage at the time of the survey. To limit the sample in this way would possibly be appropriate from the point of view of including only those individuals whose rate of pay (and presumably on-the-job training) was directly affected by a legal wage floor; nevertheless, excluding those who received higher rates of pay would reduce the number of observations substantially and possibly yield an inferior picture of the influence of experience on observed wage rates because of bias induced by truncation of the wage data. Evidently, the major thrust of the result reported here is not sensitive to whether the sample is limited by the value of the wage variable. In an unpublished paper, James E. Brown reports a substantially smaller on-the-job training component of the full wage for individuals whose 1966 job was covered by minimum wage legislation than for those whose job was not covered.[5] Brown's sample is limited to individuals reporting a wage less than $1.50 per hour in 1966 (the basic minimum was $1.25).

Variables Used in the Study. The following variables are used in the basic regression model of wage growth:

$W_{96}, W_{16} \equiv$ change in the natural logarithm of the reported wage on current or last job between 1966 and 1969 and between 1966 and 1971, respectively.

$SCH_6 \equiv$ number of years of school completed as of 1966.

$UN_9, UN_1 =$ a dummy variable equal to 1 if respondent is a member of a union in 1969 or 1971, respectively.

$AGE_6 \equiv$ the individual's age in 1966.

$S_{96}, S_{16} \equiv$ change in number of years of schooling between 1966 and 1969 or 1971, respectively.

[5] James E. Brown, "The Effects of Minimum Wages on the Later Earnings of Male Youths" (Columbus, Ohio: Ohio State University, Department of Economics, March 1980).

TABLE D2

ESTIMATES OF THE WAGE GROWTH EQUATION, 1966–1969 AND 1966–1971
(t-values in parentheses)

Dependent Variables	Independent Variables						
	SCH_6	UN_9, UN_1	AGE_6	S_{96}, S_{16}	MSP_6	MSP_9, MSP_1	EXP_6
W_{96}	−0.0083	0.23	−0.0030	0.056	−0.065	0.071	−0.0011
	(0.8)	(7.0)	(0.2)	(1.6)	(1.1)	(2.1)	(0.1)
W_{16}	0.0219	0.23	−0.016	0.035	−0.058	0.048	0.0064
	(1.8)	(5.5)	(0.9)	(1.0)	(0.9)	(1.2)	(0.5)

MSP_6, MSP_9, $MSP_1 \equiv$ a dummy variable equal to 1 if the respondent was married and living with his wife in 1966, 1969, and 1971, respectively.

$EXP_6 \equiv$ a measure of work experience before the 1966 survey—that is, 1966 less the year last attended school + 0.333 if the industry of the current job in 1966 is the same as that for the job held during the last year of school.

$COV_6 \equiv$ a variable representing the probability that the current or last job reported in the 1966 survey was subject to federal minimum wage regulation. See the discussion above.

$\Delta ST \equiv$ a variable reflecting change in enrollment status between 1966 and either 1969 or 1971; = 0 if no change, = 1 if entered school, = −1 if left school.

E_{96}, $E_{16} \equiv$ accumulated work experience between 1966 and 1969 and between 1966 and 1971, respectively. Measured as the number of weeks worked in each year multiplied by the average weekly hours worked and divided by 2,000, so that the variable is denominated in units of full-year equivalents.

(IN), (OUT) following E_{96} or E_{16} indicate whether the

Independent Variables							
COV_6	E_{96}, E_{16} (IN)	E_{96}, E_{16} (OUT)	E_{96}, E_{16} (IN) $\times COV_6$	E_{96}, E_{16} (OUT) $\times COV_6$	ΔST	$\bar{R}^2$	N
0.051 (0.4)	0.19 (2.5)	0.18 (3.4)	−0.18 (1.7)	−0.17 (2.9)	−0.16 (5.8)	0.14	1,053
−0.067 (0.2)	0.11 (1.1)	0.12 (2.2)	−0.046 (0.4)	−0.095 (1.4)	−0.16 (4.3)	0.18	596

variable measures work experience while the respondent is a full-time student or not attending school full time, respectively. Full-time student status is measured by change in reported years of school completed. If this variable increased by one year between surveys spaced a year apart, then full-time student status is assumed for the intervening year.

The Wage Growth Equation. These variables were used in the following wage growth equation:

$$\begin{aligned}\ln W_{96} = {} & \alpha_0 + \alpha_1 SCH_6 + \alpha_2 UN_9 + \alpha_3 AGE_6 + \alpha_4 S_{96} + \alpha_5 MSP_6 \\ & + \alpha_6\, MSP_9 + \alpha_7 EXP_6 + \alpha_8 COV_6 + \alpha_9 E_{96}(IN) \\ & + \alpha_{10} E_{96}(OUT) + \alpha_{11}[E_{96}(IN) \times COV_6] \\ & + \alpha_{12}[E_{96}(OUT) \times COV_6] + \alpha_{13}\Delta ST \end{aligned} \qquad \text{(D.1)}$$

Equation (D.1) is not new, and its rationale is found in Lazear's papers.[6] The crucial hypotheses for this study are $\alpha_9 > 0$, $\alpha_{10} > 0$, $\alpha_{11} < 0$, and $\alpha_{12} < 0$. Furthermore, α_{11} and α_{12} are postulated to be sufficiently negative so that the on-the-job training component of the full wage for covered workers is less than that for workers not "protected" by minimum wage legislation (see below). Equation (D.1) is easily modified to fit the 1966–1971 period by substituting the appropriate variables as listed above.

[6] Edward Lazear, "Schooling as a Wage Depressant," *Journal of Human Resources*, vol. 12, no. 1 (Spring 1977), pp. 164-76; and "Age, Experience, and Wage Growth."

TABLE D3

CALCULATION OF THE FULL WAGE RATE BY SCHOOLING AND MINIMUM WAGE COVERAGE STATUS

(dollars)

Schooling and Coverage	W_6	W_{OJT}	W_F
	Based on Wage Growth 1966–1969		
In school 1966–1969			
Covered 1966	1.44	0.14	1.58
Not covered 1966	1.24	2.29	3.53
Not in school 1966–1969			
Covered 1966	1.91	0.25	2.16
Not covered 1966	1.53	2.78	4.31
	Based on Wage Growth 1966–1971		
In school 1966–1971			
Covered 1966	1.48	0.93	2.41
Not covered 1966	1.26	1.37	2.63
Not in school 1966–1971			
Covered 1966	1.93	0.56	2.49
Not covered 1966	1.49	1.84	3.33

The results of estimating equation (D.1) are used to calculate the value of on-the-job training and the full wage as follows:

$$W_F = W_6 + W_{OJT} \qquad \text{(D.2)}$$

where W_F is the full wage, W_6 is the reported 1966 wage, and W_{OJT} is the present value of increased future wage rates associated with each hour of work experience between 1966 and either 1969 or 1971. To calculate W_{OJT}, it is assumed that experience-related wage increases are permanent for the remainder of the individual's working life, which is postulated to be forty-five years. The relevant interest rate (r) is assumed to equal 10 percent.[7] Thus

$$W_{OJT} = W_6(\alpha_{9,10} + \alpha_{11,12} \cdot COV_6) \int_{t=0}^{45} e^{-0.1t} \qquad \text{(D.3)}$$

[7] Since W_6 and the interest rate, r, are assumed constant, and since forty-five years is a sufficiently large number, the present value of training-associated wage increases is approximately equal to $1/r$ times the estimated wage change between 1966 and 1969 or 1966 and 1971.

In computing W_{OJT}, separate calculations are carried out for four groups: (1) individuals whose 1966 job was covered by minimum wage legislation and who are assumed to be in school full time while acquiring all subsequent work experience; (2) covered workers who were not full-time students; (3) noncovered workers who were full-time students; and (4) noncovered workers who were not full-time students. To illustrate, for group (1), equation (D.3) is computed setting W_6 equal to the mean reported wage in 1966 of individuals whose job was covered and who were full-time students, and using α_9 and α_{11} (setting $COV_6 = 1$); for group (4), W_6 is set equal to the mean reported wage in 1966 of individuals whose job was not covered and who were not full-time students, using α_{10} only (setting $COV_6 = 0$).

The estimates of equation (D.1) are presented in table D2. The calculations of the full wage rate and its components for the four groups of workers defined above are contained in table D3. When equation (D.1) is estimated over the 1966–1969 period, the coefficients of the variables measuring change in experience for workers not employed in a covered job in 1966 are positive, as hypothesized. It is noteworthy that, for workers not covered by minimum wage legislation, the coefficients of change in experience, α_9 and α_{10}, do not differ substantially. This means that the proportional effect of experience on earning power does not depend on whether the work experience is obtained while attending school or not. (This does not mean that the on-the-job training component of the full wage is equal for these groups, since the coefficients of the experience variables reflect the proportion of time devoted to training, not its total value.[8]) The coefficients of the variables representing the effect of minimum wage coverage on on-the-job training, α_{11} and α_{12}, are both negative. While the t-value of α_{11} is only marginally significant by conventional standards, this is not unusual in view of the high correlation between the experience variables and their products with coverage and the coverage term (COV_6) itself.

The hypotheses that α_{11} and α_{12} are negative, and sufficiently large in absolute value to result in a smaller on-the-job training component of the full wage for covered workers is confirmed, for both students and nonstudents. The difference between W_{OJT} for covered and noncovered workers is so large that, although the average reported wage is higher for covered jobs, for both students and nonstudents, the full wage is actually lower for covered than for non-

[8] See Jacob Mincer, *Schooling, Experience and Earnings* (New York: National Bureau of Economic Research, 1974).

covered employment among both groups. This reversal of wage inequality when going from W_G, the reported wage, to W_F, the full wage, is not predicted by our analysis of the influence of minimum wage regulation on on-the-job training and merits further investigation.

When equation (D.1) is estimated over the period 1966–1971, the results are similar to those obtained over the 1966–1969 period. Unfortunately, the attrition rate (due largely to the difficulty of tracing mobile respondents) from the NLS sample was extremely high among this age group, and the sample size dropped by nearly 45 percent between 1969 and 1971. While the signs of all coefficients that are statistically significant in the 1966–1969 regression are the same when equation (D.1) is estimated over the 1966–1971 period, the t-values of the coefficients of the change-in-experience variables all decline, as do their magnitudes. Nevertheless, the estimated full wage for individuals who worked on covered jobs in 1966 remains smaller than that for those who worked at jobs not covered by minimum wage legislation. The inequality between the full wage rates of the covered and noncovered groups becomes much smaller, with the ratio of the full wage of noncovered to that of covered workers falling from 2.23 to 1.09 for those who gained work experience while attending school, and from 2.00 to 1.34 for those whose experience was gained while not attending school.

Appendix E

Minimum Wage Rates in Retail Trade, 1961-1981

Table E1 details minimum wage rates and coverage in retail trade from 1961 to 1981.

TABLE E1

Minimum Wage Rates in Retail Trade (Except Eating and Drinking Places), 1961–1981
(dollars)

	Motor Vehicles	*Gas Stations*	*Other Retail Trade*							
Enterprise Sales	$250,000+	$250,000+	$250,000+			$250,000–274,999	$275,000–324,999	$325,000–499,999	$500,000–999,999	$1,000,000+
Coverage Date / *Establishment Sales*	$250,000+	$250,000+	less than $200,000	$200,000–224,999	$225,000–249,999	$250,000+				
9/3/61	a	1.00	a	a	a	a	a	a	a	1.00[b]
9/3/64	a	1.15	a	a	a	a	a	a	a	1.15[b]
9/3/65	a	1.25	a	a	a	a	a	a	a	1.25
2/1/67	1.00	1.40	a	a	a	a	a	a	1.00	1.40
2/1/68	1.15	1.60	a	a	a	a	a	a	1.15	1.60
2/1/69	1.30	1.60	a	a	a	1.30	1.30	1.30	1.30	1.60
2/1/70	1.45	1.60	a	a	a	1.45	1.45	1.45	1.45	1.60
2/1/71	1.60	1.60	a	a	a	1.60	1.60	1.60	1.60	1.60

TABLE E1 (Continued)

5/1/74	1.90	2.00	a	a	a	1.90	1.90	1.90	1.90	2.00
1/1/75	2.00	2.10	a	a	2.00	2.00	2.00	2.00	2.00	2.10
1/1/76	2.20	2.30	a	2.20	2.20	2.20	2.20	2.20	2.20	2.30
1/1/77	2.30	2.30	2.30	2.30	2.30	2.30	2.30	2.30	2.30	2.30
1/1/78	2.65	2.65	2.65	2.65	2.65	2.65	2.65	2.65	2.65	2.65
1/1/79	2.90	2.90	2.65	2.65	2.65	2.65	2.90	2.90	2.90	2.90
1/1/80	3.10	3.10	2.65	2.65	2.65	2.65	2.90	3.10	3.10	3.10
1/1/81	3.35	3.35	2.65	2.65	2.65	2.65	2.90	3.35	3.35	3.35

[a] Not covered.

[b] Retail trade minimum less than that for previously covered establishments in other industries.

SOURCES: U.S. Department of Labor, Employment Standards Administration, Division of Evaluation and Research, unpublished data, dated March 30, 1978; U.S. Department of Labor, Wage and Hour and Public Contracts Divisions, *Retail Trade: A Study to Measure the Effects of the Minimum Wage and Maximum Hours Standards of the Fair Labor Standards Act* (1967); U.S. Department of Labor, Employment Standards Administration, *Minimum Wage and Maximum Hours Standards under the Fair Labor Standards Act* (annually, 1971–1979); Commerce Clearing House, *1978 Guidebook to Federal Wage-Hours Laws* (Chicago: Commerce Clearing House, 1977).

References

Al-Salam, Nabeel; Quester, Aline; and Welch, Finis. "Some Determinants of the Level and Racial Composition of Teenage Employment." In *The Economics of Legal Minimum Wages,* edited by Simon Rottenberg. Washington, D.C.: American Enterprise Institute, forthcoming.

Ashenfelter, Orley, and Smith, Robert S. "Compliance with the Minimum Wage Law." *Journal of Political Economy* 87 (April 1979): 333–50.

Barger, Harold. *Distribution's Place in the American Economy since 1869.* Princeton, N.J.: Princeton University Press, 1955.

Becker, Gary S. "A Theory of the Allocation of Time." *Economic Journal* 75 (September 1965): 493–517.

Brown, James E. "The Effects of Minimum Wages on the Later Earnings of Male Youths." Columbus: Ohio State University, Department of Economics, March 1980.

Commerce Clearing House. *1978 Guidebook to Federal Wage-Hours Laws.* Chicago Commerce Clearing House, 1977.

Cotterill, Philip Glenn. "A Model of Labor in Retail Trade." Ph.D. dissertation, Northwestern University, 1969.

Ehrenberg, Ronald G., and Marcus, Alan. "Minimum Wage Legislation and the Educational Decisions of Youths: Perpetuation of Income Inequality across Generations?" In *The Economics of Legal Minimum Wages,* edited by Simon Rottenberg. Washington, D.C.: American Enterprise Institute, forthcoming.

Fleisher, Belton M., and Kniesner, Thomas J. *Labor Economics: Theory, Evidence, and Policy.* 2nd ed. Englewood Cliffs, N.J.: Prentice-Hall, 1980.

Freeman, Richard B. "The Effects of Demographic Factors on Age-Earnings Profiles." *Journal of Human Resources* 14 (Summer 1979): 289–318.

Freeman, Richard B., and Medoff, James L. "New Estimates of Private Sector Unionism in the United States." *Industrial and Labor Relations Review* 32 (January 1979): 143–74.

Goldberger, A. S. "Best Linear Unbiased Prediction in a Linear Regression Model." *Journal of the American Statistical Association* 57 (June 1962): 369–75.

Johnson, Harry G. "Minimum Wage Laws: A General Equilibrium Analysis." *The Canadian Journal of Economics* 2 (November 1970): 539–61.

Katz, Arnold. "Teenage Employment Effects of State Minimum Wages." *Journal of Human Resources* 8 (Spring 1973): 250–56.

King, Allen. "Minimum Wages and the Secondary Labor Market." *Southern Economic Journal* 41 (October 1974): 215–19.

Lazear, Edward. "Age, Experience, and Wage Growth." *American Economic Review* 66 (September 1976): 548–58.

Lazear, Edward. "The Narrowing of Black-White Wage Differentials Is Illusory." *American Economic Review* 69 (September 1969): 553–64.

Lazear, Edward. "Schooling as a Wage Depressant." *Journal of Human Resources* 12 (Spring 1977): 164–76.

Lebergott, Stanley. "Labor Force and Employment, 1800–1960." In *Output, Employment, and Productivity in the United States after 1800,* Conference on Research in Income and Wealth, Studies in Income and Wealth, 30. New York: National Bureau of Economic Research, 1966. (Distributed by Columbia University Press.)

Lewis, H. G. *Unionism and Relative Wages in the United States.* Chicago: University of Chicago Press, 1963.

Mattila, J. Peter. "The Impact of Minimum Wages on Teenage Schooling and on the Part-Time/Full-Time Employment of Youths." In *The Economics of Legal Minimum Wages,* edited by Simon Rottenberg. Washington, D.C.: American Enterprise Institute, forthcoming.

McCulloch, J. Huston. "The Effect of a Minimum Wage Law in the Labor Intensive Search," *Canadian Journal of Economics* 7 (May 1974): 316–19.

Mincer, Jacob. *Schooling, Experience and Earnings.* New York: National Bureau of Economic Research, 1974.

Mincer, Jacob. "Unemployment Effects of Minimum Wages." *Journal of Political Economy* 84 (August 1976): S87–S104.

Mincer, Jacob, and Leighton, Linda. "Effect of Minimum Wages on Human Capital Formation," Working Paper No. 441. Cambridge, Mass.: National Bureau of Economic Research, February 1980.

Nadiri, M. Ishaq, and Rosen, Sherwin. *A Disequilibrium Model of Demand for Factors of Production.* National Bureau of Economic Research General Series No. 99. New York: National Bureau of Economic Research, 1973. (Distributed by Columbia University Press.)

National Longitudinal Survey of Young Men. Columbus: Ohio State University, Center for Human Resource Research.

Ragan, James. "Minimum Wages and Youth Labor Market." *Review of Economics and Statistics* 59 (May 1977): 129–36.

Schwartzman, David. "The Growth of Sales per Man-Hour in Retail Trade, 1929–1963." In *Production and Productivity in the Service Industries,* edited by Victor R. Fuchs. New York: National Bureau of Economic Research, 1969. (Distributed by Columbia University Press.)

Tauchen, George E. "Some Evidence on Cross-Sector Effects of the Minimum Wage." Unpublished paper, July 1978. Drawn from a Ph.D. dissertation, University of Minnesota, 1978.

U.S. Bureau of the Census. *Census of Business, 1954.* Vol 1. *Retail Trade—Summary Statistics.* 1958.

U.S. Bureau of the Census. *Census of Population,* 1930, 1940, 1950, 1960, 1970.

U.S. Bureau of the Census. *Census of Retail Trade, 1972.* Vol. 1. *Summary and Subject Statistics.* 1976.

U.S. Bureau of the Census. *Current Population Reports.* Series P-25, No. 72. April 1978.

U.S. Bureau of the Census. *Current Population Survey, March 1978.* Public Use Sample.

U.S. Bureau of the Census. *Historical Statistics of the United States, Colonial Times to 1970.* 1975.

U.S. Bureau of the Census. *Statistical Abstract of the United States, 1979.* 1979.

U.S. Congress, House of Representatives, Subcommittee on Labor Standards of the Committee on Education and Labor. *Hearings on Various Bills Regarding Minimum Wage Legislation.* 86th Congress, 2nd session, March 16–April 13, 1960, p. 67.

U.S. Department of Commerce, Bureau of Economic Analysis. *Survey of Current Business.* Various issues.

U.S. Department of Commerce, Office of Business Economics. *The National Income and Product Accounts of the United States, 1929–65.* 1967.

U.S. Department of Commerce, Office of Business Economics. *The National Income and Product Accounts of the United States, 1964–67.* 1971.

U.S. Department of Labor. *Employment and Training Report of the President, 1979.* 1980.

U.S. Department of Labor, Bureau of Labor Statistics. *Employment and Earnings, United States.* Various years.

U.S. Department of Labor, Bureau of Labor Statistics. *Employee Earnings in Retail Trade in October 1956.* Bulletin 1220 and 1220-1 to 1220-7. July 1957.

U.S. Department of Labor, Bureau of Labor Statistics. "The Fair Labor Standards Act: Changes of Four Decades." *Monthly Labor Review* 102 (July 1979): 10–16.

U.S. Department of Labor, Bureau of Labor Statistics. *Handbook of Labor Statistics, 1978.* 1979.

U.S. Department of Labor, Employment Standards Administration. *Minimum Wage and Maximum Hours Standards under the Fair Labor Standards Act.* Annually 1971–1979.

U.S. Department of Labor, Wage and Hour and Public Contracts Divisions. *Retail Trade: An Interim Study of the Effects of the 1961 Amendments.* 1966.

U.S. Department of Labor, Wage and Hour and Public Contracts Divisions. *Retail Trade: A Study of the Effects of the 1961 Amendments.* 1967.

U.S. Department of Labor, Wage and Hour and Public Contracts Divisions. *Retail Trade: A Study to Measure the Effects of the Minimum Wage and Maximum Hours Standards of the Fair Labor Standards Act.* 1967.

Welch, Finis. "Effects of Cohort Size on Earnings: The Baby Boom Babies' Financial Bust." *Journal of Political Economy* 87 (October 1979): S65–S98.

Welch, Finis. "Minimum Wage Legislation in the United States." In *Evaluating the Labor Market Effects of Social Programs,* edited by Orley Ashenfelter and James Blum, pp. 1–38. Princeton, N.J.: Princeton University Industrial Relations Section, 1977.

Welch, Finis. *Minimum Wages: Issues and Evidence,* Washington, D.C.: American Enterprise Institute, 1978.

Wessels, Walter J. "The Effect of Minimum Wages on Fringe Benefits: An Expanded Model." *Economic Inquiry* 18 (April 1980): 293–313.

White, Kenneth J. *Shazam: An Econometrics Computer Program.* Version 2.0. Houston: Rice University, Department of Economics, September 1977.

Willis, Robert J., and Rosen, Sherwin. "Education and Self-Selection." *Journal of Political Economy* 87 (October 1979): S7–S36.

Zucker, A. "Minimum Wages and the Demand for Low Wage Labor." *Quarterly Journal of Economics,* May 1973, 267–79.

A NOTE ON THE BOOK

The typeface used for the text of this book is
Palatino, designed by Hermann Zapf.
The type was set by
Hendricks-Miller Typographic Company, Washington, D.C.
BookCrafters, Incorporated, of Chelsea, Michigan, printed
and bound the book, using Glatfelter paper.
The cover and format were designed by Pat Taylor,
and the figures were drawn by Hördur Karlsson.
The manuscript was edited by Robert L. Faherty
and by Anne Gurian of the AEI Publications staff.